W9-BRY-477

EASTER EGGS
BY THE DOZENS!

FUN AND CREATIVE
EGG-DECORATING
PROJECTS
FOR ALL
AGES!

RHONDA MASSINGHAM HART

A Storey Publishing Book

STOREY

Storey Communications, Inc.
Schoolhouse Road
Pownal, Vermont 05261

Freeport Public Library
Freeport, Illinois

Cover design by Wanda Harper Joyce

Cover illustration by Patti Delmonte

Text design and production by Wanda Harper Joyce

Illustrations by Alison Kolesar

Indexed by Nan No Badgett

Copyright © 1993 Rhonda Massingham Hart

All rights reserved. No part of this book may be reproduced without written permission from the publisher, except by a reviewer who may quote brief passages or reproduce illustrations in a review with appropriate credits; nor may any part of this book be reproduced, stored in a retrieval system, or transmitted in any form or by any means — electronic, mechanical, photocopying, recording, or other — without written permission from the publisher.

The information in this book is true and complete to the best of our knowledge. All recommendations are made without guarantee on the part of the author or Storey Communications, Inc. The author and publisher disclaim any liability in connection with the use of this information. For additional information, please contact Storey Communications, Inc., Schoolhouse Road, Pownal, Vermont 05261.

Printed in the United States by Capitol City Press
First Printing, January 1993

Library of Congress Cataloging-in-Publication Data
Hart, Rhonda Massingham.
    Easter eggs — by the dozens! : fun and creative egg-decorating projects for all ages! / Rhonda Massingham Hart.
        p.   cm.
    Includes bibliographical references and index.
    ISBN 0-88266-808-0 (pbk.)
    1. Egg decoration.   I. Title.
TT896.7.H37   1992
745.594'4 — dc20
                                                    92-53807
                                                    CIP

DEDICATION

Family is family,
    the chain never ends.
They stand by you always,
    and you stand by them.
How fortunate are we
    when we see our kin
As more than a family,
    but as our best friends.

To my cousin, my friend
(and a good egg),
Debbie Massingham Wilson

Special thanks to Pam Art for her ARTistic inspiration, and Amy Logan for her crafty ideas, constant enthusiasm, and unlimited tolerance. Thanks also to Bernadette Wagner for so generously sharing her abundant creative talents in egg dyeing and pysanky.

931979

INTRODUCTION

aster is among the most cherished of Christian holidays, and for centuries, brightly adorned eggs have symbolized this special day. Decorated eggs have been discovered that date as far back as the fourth century. The egg, however, was an almost universal symbol of spring and rebirth long before Christians adopted it. But why eggs?

Cheap and plentiful, eggs were available to everyone. The transformation of the seemingly lifeless shell into a new living being was an obvious sign of magical power. Early pagan feasts revered the egg as proof of the continuity of nature. Early Egyptian and Chinese celebrations included eggs. Well before the time of Christ, Persia celebrated the new year with the Feast of the Red Egg, and red-dyed eggs were favored throughout much of the Middle Ages. Eventually red, being the color of love, blood, and victory, was used to decorate eggs, the symbol of rebirth and magic, to represent the resurrection of Jesus Christ.

As old and rich as the traditions of Easter are, those of the decorated egg are even more so. Such an old and diverse history generates many variations. There are at least as many ways to decorate eggs as there are cultures that partake in this time-honored custom.

Some of the techniques for decorating eggs are simple enough for children to enjoy. Others are complex means to an artistic end. Some of the eggs are destined to be eaten as the spoils of the successful Easter egg hunter, while others are carefully wrapped and saved as precious keepsakes, often passed down through generations as family heirlooms. Whether you intend to create a colorful reward for a small searcher or a masterpiece for all time, you will find a way to do it in the pages that follow.

GETTING STARTED

Before getting out the dyes, do-dads, and other decorations there are a few preliminaries to consider. They include gathering the proper equipment and supplies, choosing the eggs, deciding whether to cook the eggs or to remove the insides.

EQUIPMENT & SUPPLIES

The supplies you will need for decorating eggs depends on the technique you will be using. Special materials for individual methods are listed with the instructions for each project. Here are the basics.

Eggs. OK, this seems a little obvious, but there really are some things to know here. For many projects you will get better results if you use white eggs. Brown eggs don't seem to accept many dyes as well as white eggs do, and the brown shell affects the color. Other colored eggs, for instance green or blue Araucana chicken eggs, have similar problems, but produce unique results.

Start with eggs that are fresh and absolutely clean and free of cracks or other irregularities in the shell. Store-bought eggs are usually coated with mineral oil to help replace nature's protective coating lost during processing. The oil protects the eggs and extends the shelf life, but it seals the pores, giving a slick finish that tends to reject dyes. Hold each egg up to a light source to check for fine cracks or mysterious blotches. Don't vigorously scrub when cleaning as this can cause scraped spots that won't take dye and result in uneven color.

To properly cleanse eggs, rinse them in a pint of warm water mixed with one tablespoon of white vinegar. Allow to air dry or pat dry with a clean, soft

C
H
A
P
T
E
R
1

3

Eggs

Glass, enamel, or steel pan

Wooden, stainless steel, or silver spoons

Dye (or other coloring agent)

Cups (for each color dye)

White vinegar (dye additive)

Sharp instrument to pierce shell

Egg rack

Covering for work area

Other materials you may find useful include, but are not limited to: rubber bands, pencils, wax, glue, sponges, crepe paper, kistka (see Pysanky), razor blades, old pantyhose, turnips, construction paper, ribbon, yarn, leaves, flowers, macaroni, glitter, Styrofoam, fabric scraps, beads, cotton balls, wiggle-eyes, scissors, miniature figurines, sugar, egg whites, egg molds, icing, cake decorating tubes, hole punch, and jewelry-making supplies. Such a diverse and intriguing list adds up to a wide variety of sometimes whimsical, often clever, and always beautiful Easter eggs.

cloth. Avoid soaps and detergents, they are too harsh. It is important to keep your hands free of grease whenever handling the eggs. Wash your hands often, in between each step if necessary, and forget about hand lotion until you have put away your "eggworks."

Utensils. Handling such a fragile artist's canvas requires skill and special utensils. Even hard-boiled eggs have special requirements. Always use a glass, enamel, or steel pan to cook eggs. Utensils made of iron or aluminum will react chemically with the eggshell in a way that prevents it from taking dye, so use only wooden, stainless steel, or silver spoons to stir dyes or to immerse eggs.

For dyeing you will need a separate container for each color. This could be a cup or small bowl of glass, porcelain, or plastic. Recycle paper or Styrofoam drink cups into egg dye baths. White vinegar is often added to many dyes.

If the egg is not to be cooked then the insides should be blown from the shell. This step requires nothing more than a sharp instrument, such as a nail, darning needle, or bamboo skewer and a bowl.

For many projects, an egg rack is virtually indispensable. This is where the eggs rest when drying or when you need both hands. Make a simple, inexpensive rack by driving one-inch nails through a piece of board or heavy cardboard in triangles set about 1½ inches apart. Each triangle will support an egg with the least amount of contact possible, and without smudging wet dye or paint as it dries. Push triangles of toothpicks into a block of Styrofoam for a similar stand, or turn over an egg carton. Pizza lovers can collect and use the three-pronged, plastic box-supports from pizza parlors. Turned upside-down, these make ideal individual egg stands. Ring stands, such as napkin rings, shower curtain rings, or circles cut from paper towel or toilet-paper rolls are also useful. They should not be used for drying dripping wet, dyed eggs, however, as the dye will puddle where the ring meets the egg and leave a visible ring.

Protection. While decorating eggs is not inherently dangerous, for many projects some type of protection for the work area is crucial. Often in the process of creating a single object of beauty, we also find ourselves splashing, spilling, dripping, and just generally making a darned good mess. For dyeing, painting, or gluing projects play it safe by spreading out an old vinyl tablecloth, some large plastic garbage liners (cut open to cover twice the area), or several layers of newspaper. Have a clean, damp cloth on hand to quickly wipe up any accidents, and be aware of which products you are using that might leave permanent stains, such as many felt-tip markers or fabric dyes.

TO COOK OR NOT TO COOK

Whether or not you boil eggs before decorating them depends on the destiny of the eggs. Those bound for an egg hunt should be cooked. Boiling, however, allows a small amount of water to penetrate the porous shell. The water may seep out later and ruin the design. Eggs to be kept as keepsakes are usually blown because the hollow shell will keep forever — or at least until someone fumbles it.

For the successful egg hunter, only a perfectly cooked egg will do. Fortunately, boiling an egg to perfection is easy. While improperly cooked eggs crack, ooze, or taste and feel like rubber, those cooked as follows will be flawless every time.

The Perfect Hardboiled Egg

1. Choose a pan (glass, enamel, or steel) large enough to hold all the eggs to be cooked at one time without crowding or allowing them to bump into each other. Be sure it is totally grease free.

2. To help prevent cracking, bring the eggs to room temperature.

3. Place the eggs in the pan and cover with cold water. Fill the pan one inch over the tops of the eggs.

4. Bring to a boil, and remove from heat immediately.

5. Cover and allow to stand for 20–25 minutes, as the hot water gently and evenly cooks the eggs.

6. Remove the eggs and rinse with cold water. This not only cools the eggs, but causes the cooked whites to shrink away from the shells, making them easier to peel.

(**Note**: Saved and cooled, the egg-boiling water is great for houseplants.)

Hollow eggs have the advantage as ornaments because they are light-weight and can be displayed in many ways. They are very fragile and must be handled with the tender, loving care such keepsakes deserve.

How to Blow an Egg

Be sure to have someone take your photograph! It's a safe bet that you will probably never look sillier than when you are trying to blow the insides out of an egg. But it is a noble endeavor, so don't let a mere temporary lapse of dignity sway you from the deed.

Let the egg rest in an egg carton, both to steady it and to cushion the bottom. Center a small nail, darning needle, or other sharp object over the end of the egg and gently, but firmly tap with a hammer. Turn the egg over and tap a small hole in the other end as well. (The tinier the holes the better, they need be no bigger in diameter than a toothpick, but even oversized holes can be covered with a dot of wax or a small piece of glued colored paper.) Push the sharp instrument into the bottom hole a short distance and agitate the insides to break the membrane surrounding the yolk. Now seal your lips around one end of the egg and blow! Continue until you can force air through the hole at the opposite end.

Though you may feel like a six-year-old at his first trumpet lesson, this simple approach usually works. You may have to stop occasionally to pull a glob of egg out of the exit hole. If you happen to raise chickens, you may notice that homegrown eggs tend to have tougher shells. Keep a paper towel handy for glob-pulling, and tap a little harder with the hammer if you need to, but always remember to handle eggs carefully.

Whether to blow the eggs prior to or after decorating is a matter of personal choice. Blowing them beforehand makes them difficult to dye. Hollow eggs float. Rather than sinking passively to the bottom of the dye bath, they bob around as if looking for a way to get out. They must be held down or weighted and turned frequently; a lot of bother. This is fine as long as the egg is only being dyed one color, but during any subsequent baths dye will leak back out through the holes to foul the intended color. On the other hand, there is the tragic waste of dyeing four coats of color over an elaborately decorated egg only to "oops" during the blowing stage. It's a gamble. Veteran egg dyers prefer to take their chances and empty the eggs out after dyeing. Of course, if you are working on a project that does not involve dyeing, such as one of the many "glue-ons" described later, it is best to blow the egg out before decorating. Always let a blown egg drain and dry completely before painting, gluing, or filling. Seeping whites will ruin your work.

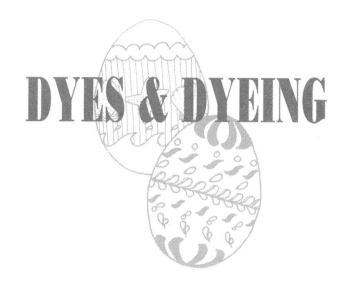

DYES & DYEING

Probably the most common way of coloring eggs is to immerse them in a dye bath. They may be dyed only one shade or have several coats applied. Often the dye is blocked from reaching certain parts of the egg by a barrier, such as wax, rubber bands, or leaves. The varieties of dye and methods of applying them are practically limitless.

Of major importance in choosing a dye is whether or not the decorated egg will be eaten. Some dyes are edible and others are not. Those that are not may even be toxic.

EDIBLE DYES

An eggshell serves many purposes. It was designed to protect the developing embryo within a fertilized egg. To do this the covering must be rigid and strong enough to withstand the internal pressures as well as a certain amount of external interference. It also must allow for the free exchange of gases — carbon dioxide out and oxygen in. To do this the shell must be porous. Thousands of tiny pores dot the surface of an egg, and along with allowing gases to pass back and forth, they also let water pass through. And dyes. Often dyes penetrate into the insides of an egg. This makes it very important not to confuse edible dyes with inedible dyes when coloring eggs that will be eaten.

Any dyed eggs to be eaten must be colored only with nontoxic dyes. Inexpensive Easter egg dyes are available in supermarkets every year just before Easter. Food colorings also work well and allow you to custom mix shades, though the colors tend to bleed if the dyed egg gets even a drop of

DYE RECIPE ONE

1. Collect (or go to a yarn store or spinner's supply store and buy) the raw dye material.

2. Wash collected material thoroughly in warm water and pick out any foreign matter.

3. Finely chop or break the dye material into small pieces. The amount used will determine the depth of the shade produced. While raw materials vary greatly, a generous handful per cup of water should be enough.

4. Place in the pot, and add just enough water to cover. Use a glass or wooden stirrer.

5. Heat to a low boil, and cook until the water reaches the desired color. This could take only a few minutes or up to an hour depending on the raw material used and the shade you want. Note: the shade on the egg will be much lighter than color of dyebath.

6. Strain through a fine sieve or cheesecloth into another container, and add a teaspoon or two of white vinegar (except for onion skins). Store in the refrigerator in a closed glass container.

7. Follow directions below for the dyeing process.

water on it. And there is a vast realm of homemade dyes. Many are safe to eat. Many aren't. Some edible homemade dyes to try include beet juice, onion skins, berry juice, boiled spinach, and coffee. Read more about these types of coloring agents in the section on natural dyes.

INEDIBLE DYES

Here the list expands to include almost anything that imparts color. Commercially available fabric dyes come in a rainbow of rich shades from bright to pastel. Once prepared they can be reused for many dozens of eggs before losing their potency. They can be stored for several seasons in covered glass containers. Use care when handling such dyes, because unlike food colorings, these dyes are colorfast. They will stain clothing, tablecloths, and other fabrics permanently. The hot-water bath dyes make wax-resist dyeing nearly impossible as it melts the wax.

The best dyes to use for coloring eggs are those specially formulated for use on eggs. These are aniline dyes available in a range of beautiful, long-lasting colors. They are available through specialty supply houses. (See Appendix for source lists.)

NATURAL DYES

With so many ready-to-use dyes available you may wonder, "why bother?" But nature's palette of rich hues and the endless variations provide a glorious reward for the extra effort. Besides, for many it is a part of the tradition and part of the fun. Gathering and processing natural dyes brings out the alchemist in us as well as the artist.

The search for natural dyes can begin at your back door or flower box. But be forewarned, not every lovely flower reproduces its shade in a dye. The soft lavender of lilac blossoms, for example, yield an off-green color. Sometimes it is the stem or root of a plant that produces the best color. One example is madder root. It has been cultivated for centuries as a standard of red dyes. Some ingredients are best used dried or powdered, others as an extract, and still others must be fresh. Often fresh plants yield the most vivid shades.

For a sampling of the dyes nature has to offer, refer to the table on page 10.

As anyone who has ever battled grass or mulberry stains knows, this list is by no means complete. There are hundreds of dye sources to be found all around us. Part of the fun of using them is the experimentation and discovery of what works and what doesn't.

Using natural dyes on eggs is nothing new. Until the 1950s they were the only dyes for egg decorating. Volumes have been written on the subject of preparing and using homemade dyes (generally intended for fabric), and ancient recipes for dye-making can still be used today. Two simple recipes are included on pages 8 and 9.

THE DYEING PROCESS

Dyeing eggs may be as simple as applying one coat of solid color or as complex as applying several overlapping shades in a wax-resist batik pattern. The same steps are followed for virtually every case.

First, decide whether the egg is to be dyed raw, hard boiled, or blown. Hollow eggs are the most difficult to dye. In order for them to take color evenly, they must be held down and continually turned in the dyebath until the desired color is reached. Eventually enough dye will seep in through the blow holes to sink it.

How long does it take to dye an egg? That depends on the type of dye being used and the shade of color desired. Soft pastels of commercial kits or food-coloring dyes can be achieved in minutes, while deep, rich shades may take from an hour or more to overnight. The darker the shade, the longer time it takes.

Be sure the egg is at room temperature and absolutely free of grease. This includes traces of oil from fingerprints. A quick wipe with white vinegar or rubbing alcohol will remove any smears.

Prepare the dye according to package directions or recipe. Be sure to use hot, warm, or cold water as per instructions. For deeper shades, use more dye per cup of water. For the darkest shades, such as black, double the amount.

Pour dye into a cup and add a teaspoon or two of white vinegar.

Use a spoon or wire egg holder (supplied in egg-dyeing kits) to gently lower the egg into the dye. A raw or cooked egg can rest in the cup until it reaches the shade you want, but a hollow egg must be kept in motion. The spoon may remain in the cup.

Single-colored eggs should air dry on an egg rack before further handling. Eggs undergoing multiple baths can be patted (not rubbed) dry with a clean, soft cloth. You can produce a two-toned egg by holding the egg in a wire egg-holder in the dye only up to the level of the wire holder. Let the egg dry on an eggrack, wet-end down to prevent the dye from running. When dry, turn the egg over, and dye the other end in another shade. You can take this idea a step further by first dyeing the egg a light shade, then over-dyeing first one end and then the other in two different shades. Choose colors that combine to create a third appealing shade, such as red and blue over yellow, to make a three-toned egg.

In dyeing multiple coats, remember that the first coat will affect the color of the second and so on. For example, to get a green color over a yellow base, use a blue dye as the second coat. Always dye the lightest shade first and work toward the darkest color last. For instance, starting with a white egg, first dye a yellow coat, then red, and finally black. Small bits of color that don't warrant an entire dye bath can be applied with a paintbrush.

Occasionally an egg will not accept color. This is not uncommon with duck and goose eggs. Try adding extra vinegar. Don't let an errant egg frustrate you. It may be perfectly suited for another type of decorating, such as painting, marbling, or glue-on decoration.

THE FINISHING TOUCH

Once an egg is dyed and dried, you may wish to add a finish to protect the color and add a lustrous gloss. This is an especially good idea over food colorings, watercolors, or others that tend to smudge or run. Spray shellac or varnish produces a strong, slick, shiny finish. After the egg has dried completely, let the egg rest on a three-point egg stand and hold the can at least six inches from the egg to avoid creating thick, uneven spots or dripping

DYE RECIPE TWO

Dye Recipe Two is really just a shortcut of Dye Recipe One. Since the result is dyed, cooked eggs, it is customary to use only food-safe dyes, so that the eggs may be eaten.

1. Follow the first four steps as for Dye Recipe One.

2. Add eggs to pan. Do not crowd.

3. Bring the water to a boil, then reduce heat and simmer for 15 to 20 minutes. Remove eggs and rinse.

An old Saxon method of egg decorating, called "Sassy Eggs," calls for laying down a piece of cloth, covering it with onion skins, arranging small flowers or leaves on top, and finally setting an egg on top of all that. The cloth was drawn over and around the egg and fastened into a tight bundle. The egg was then boiled in water, sometimes containing coffee grounds.

MORE INEDIBLE EGG COLORINGS

Paints, including water colors, acrylics, poster paints, etc., and

Inks, such as India ink and those sold for stamp pads, impart crisp, clear, solid colors.

Felt-tip pens, in dozens of colors with tips of different shapes and thicknesses, make creating colorful designs child's play.

Fabric paints and writers come in pens or bottles that allow you to draw or paint straight from the container. In shades from neon to pastel to metallic or glittery, they can be smoothed or piped into a raised line to add an interesting three-dimensional texture.

Crepe paper dye. The process can be messy, but the results are beautiful. Make dye by soaking a 20-inch square of crepe tissue in a cup of warm water in a medium-sized bowl for about two minutes, or until most of the color has come out of the paper. Squeeze the wet paper out into the bowl. Make colors more intense by using more paper or less water.

NATURAL DYES

Color	Substance	Comments
Red	Beet juice	
	Red onion peel (*Allium* sp.)	With vinegar
	Safflower (*Carthamus tinctoria*)	
	Pokeberries (*Phytolacca americana*)	Crimson
Orange	Yellow onion peel	Steeped slightly
	Marigold blossoms	
	Dandelion root	
Yellow	Yellow onion peel	
	Turmeric or ground saffron root	
	Sumac berries (*Rhys glabra*)	Dark yellow-tan
	Mullein blossoms	
	Marigold blossoms	
	Fennel	
	Grape leaves	
Green	Spinach	
	Nettle leaves and roots	
	Combination of yellow and blue natural dyes	
Blue	Blueberries	
	Larkspur blossoms	
	Buckwheat	
Purple	Red cabbage	Pale lavender
	Elderberries	
	Combination of red and blue natural dyes	
Brown	Common hops (*Humulus lupuli*)	
	Tea	
	Coffee	
	Hickory nut hulls	Light brown
	Butternut hulls	
	Red onion skins	
Black	Blackberry shoots	

puddles. Spray a light coating evenly over the surface of the egg. Be sure to spray in a well-ventilated area, and to protect your work surface with newspapers or plastic garbage bags.

Liquid varnish can be gently rubbed on with a soft, clean piece of cloth. It takes only a few drops per egg.

Fingernail polish makes a great finish. It is fast drying, tough, and shiny. Pearly or glittery polishes add a luminous or sparkling touch.

Salad oil, baby oil, or mineral oil offer alternatives to shiny, hard-shell finishes. A few drops of either of these, gently rubbed onto the dyed egg with a tissue, protects the color from moisture, and lends a soft, subtle glow.

SYMBOLISM

From ancient pagan ceremonies to egg rolling contests on the White House lawn, decorated eggs have been a part of the spring celebrations of scores of cultures for hundreds of years. Over time, colors, symbols, and designs came to have traditionally recognized meanings. A gift of a decorated egg was meant to bestow the good wishes of the maker onto the recipient. By incorporating certain colors and symbols into the design, one could express very specific messages through the beautiful, and often elaborate, imagery.

COLORS

In the introduction of this book, it was mentioned that the color red had become important in egg decorating tradition. Ah, but this is only the tip of the rainbow. Other colors too, because of their scarcity as dyes or their associations in nature, came to acquire their own individual meanings.

Manufactured from the shells of tiny shellfish, purple was one of the rarest and most expensive dyes. At one time it was available only to the rich and powerful, and later was associated with royalty. It became popular not only because of its exuberant shades, but also because it was a way of displaying wealth and influence. Green is the color of the earth. It stands not only for growth but for healthy and abundant crops. Blue stands for good health, and brown symbolizes contentment. Black is considered the color of remembrance. White symbolizes purity and grace. Yellow, long honored as the color of Chinese royalty, in part gained this stature through its symbolism of spirituality. Pink stands for success, and orange confesses attraction or desire.

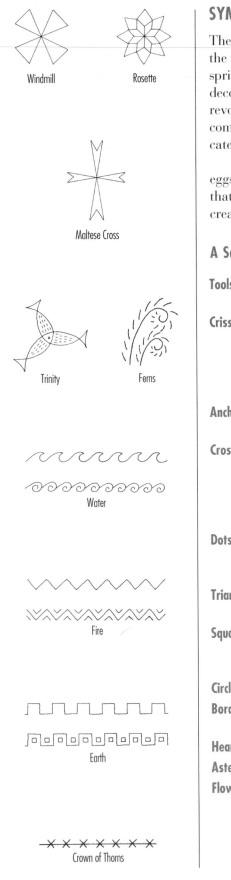

Windmill

Rosette

Maltese Cross

Trinity

Ferns

Water

Fire

Earth

Crown of Thorns

SYMBOLS

The symbolism incorporated into decorated eggs is fascinating. Throughout the world different symbols have become synonymous with the heralding of spring and later the celebration of Easter. Since the originators of many egg-decorating customs were primarily country folk, most of their symbols revolved around rural life. Agricultural, religious and fertility themes still are common. Many designs are simple geometric shapes, while others are intricate and complex.

Some traditional symbols, common to the fabulous Ukrainian Easter eggs and others, are shown and "translated" for you here. But bear in mind that the design of *your* Easter eggs is a personal expression of your own creativity and need not be limited by traditional meanings.

A Sampler of Traditional Symbols:

Tools, rake, ladder, scythe, windmill. Symbols of a good harvest.

Crisscross or checkerboard. Symbolizes the net Jesus referred to when He spoke of His disciples as "fishers of men." Often used as filler.

Anchor. Early Christian symbol of salvation.

Cross. Associated with the Christian church today, but its origins are in pagan ceremony. There are many variations. Symbolizes resurrection and eternal life.

Dots or small circles. Teardrops or, when used en masse as filler, the stars of heaven.

Triangle, cloverleaf. Three-sided symbols represent the trinity.

Square. The four directions — north, south, east, west; the four seasons; or the four winds.

Circle. Infinity, all.

Borders or Ribbons. Un-ending lines mean everlasting life, eternity.

Hearts. Love, devotion.

Asterisk. Spirituality.

Flowers. Love, charity, and goodwill.

Poppy. Good fortune; also represents the sun.

Rose. Everlasting love and caring.

Twigs, leaves, trees, and vines. Life and growth.

Evergreens. Eternal youth, good health.

Wheat. Bountiful harvest, crop protection.

Oak leaves. Virility.

Ring of thorns. The crown of Christ.

Other plant symbols. Good harvest, the return of spring, and renewal.

Hen. Fertility to women.

Rooster. Virility to men.

Other birds. Express hope that wishes are fulfilled.

Lion. Valor and strength.

Dog or wolf (or just teeth). Loyalty and protection.

Horse or deer. Prosperity and good health.

Lamb. Peace or follower of Christ.

Fish. Early Christian symbol for Jesus.

Snake. A symbol of warning.

Spiders, butterflies. Common designs of country life.

Sun and stars. The life force, good fortune, and growing or striving upward.

Of course, a design does not have to be traditionally associated with eggs to find its way onto one. There are wonderful designs all around us, many of which make interesting subjects for egg decorating. Patterns common to other cultures make for exotic eggs. Historic symbols, such as a family coat-of-arms, cattle brands, or military or professional insignia, may have special significance for someone on your egg gift list. Add a unique touch to someone's table by creating a one-of-a-kind Easter egg in their china pattern. Company logos, favorite flowers or pets, or images depicting a hobby or accomplishment will certainly delight anyone who receives such a thoughtful token.

Patterns with simple geometric patterns give some of the best results on eggs. Quilt patterns are a great example; they make the transition from fabric to eggshell splendidly.

Another intriguing example is the richly symbolic hex signs which so commonly graced turn-of-the-century barns. These sometimes simple, sometimes intricate, always colorful Amish symbols represent wishes of good fortune. Hex signs make beautiful medallions on eggs or the perfect finishing touch for either end of the egg.

Justice

Sunshine

Rain

12-Point Star
'Wisdom'

8-Point Star
'Good Luck'

Churn Dash

Sisters Choice

Le Moyne Star

Seesaw

Featherwreath

Shoofly

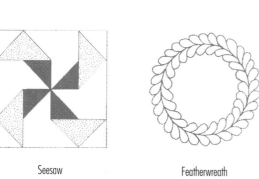

The patterns and hidden meanings of quilting and hex sign designs complement the rich symbolism of traditional egg decorating.

DIVIDING THE EGG

Although symbols and designs may certainly be scattered randomly over the surface of the egg, very often they are worked into a pattern that starts by visually dividing the egg into sections. Dividing lines can be lightly drawn in pencil, colored pencil, or crayon to serve as guidelines. It is much easier to follow the guidelines when painting or applying hot wax than to work freehand. But even the steadiest hand can waver when drawing those guidelines. How can you make them straight and perfect every time?

Two of the most valuable things the egg artist can add to his or her art arsenal are rubber bands and masking tape. Position a snug fitting rubber band wherever you envision the lines of your design, and use as you would a ruler to draw the lines. Masking tape can be used in the same way, though you may first need to cut it into narrow strips. Either of these "rulers" will make drawing flawless lines nearly effortless.

Following are some basic patterns to help divide the egg as you begin the design. Symbols, colors, and embellishments will individualize your egg.

The first step in creating an elaborate design is often to divide the egg into sections.

WORKING WITH WAX

 ome of the most elaborate and beautiful egg designs are created using what is known as the wax-resist dyeing method, or batik. There are several variations, but the basic technique is simple: apply melted wax to the parts of the egg's pattern you do not want to take the dye, dye the egg, and repeat through as many dyebaths as you wish there to be colors. For instance, beginning with a white egg, wax in all parts of the design that are to remain white, then dip the egg into its first dye bath, let's say yellow. When the egg is dry, apply wax to the areas that you want to stay yellow, then dunk it in a second color of dye, this time red. If you were to stop here the final product would be a red egg with white and yellow markings. You can continue however, for as many as five dye baths, or stop at just one. The wax is left on through each successive dye bath and removed all at once in one final step.

Dye cannot penetrate the wax, and only the waxless portions of the egg will take on the color of any given dye bath. The steps of waxing and dyeing result in a multicolored pattern. Always dye the lightest shade first, and graduate to the darker colors since each successive coat will affect the unwaxed part of the egg. For example, the unwaxed part of a yellow-dyed egg will turn greenish when dipped in blue.

Batik has been a popular method for decorating many things, from eggs to fabric, since the Dark Ages. Sophisticated, ornate screens found in India date back to the eighth century, establishing that the process had already become highly refined by that time. Likewise, it has been practiced throughout the Orient and Indonesia for hundreds of years. But since the Far East has little history of *egg* decorating, the course of how this ingenious dyeing technique traveled from there to places like the Baltic and Ukraine, where it was adopted, mastered, and perfected for egg decorating, is a historical blur. Some theorize that world-weary soldiers discovered the lovely art as they passed through these regions on their return from the Crusades. It is easy to imagine how they could have been so taken with it that they happily carried this exotic new idea back home.

Wax-resist, in all its variations, is but one way of using wax to decorate eggs. Other methods involve using different types of wax to achieve various effects. In batik the wax is used to create a dyed-on pattern. After the egg undergoes its final dye bath, the wax is removed. In other wax-decorating methods, such as wax-dripping, wax-relief, and wax-scratching, colored wax is an integral part of the finished design.

SPECIAL WAX-RESIST DYEING METHODS

Here are two wax-resist dyeing methods that can add new dimensions to the results you can achieve with dye. The first is a water wash and the second an orange dye wash.

A water wash can be used to get the effects of three different shades from a single cup of dye. After the initial wax design is applied to the eggshell, dye the egg until it takes on a light shade of the color you are dyeing. It may be further lightened by rinsing the egg briefly in a cup of clean water. Pat the egg dry and continue waxing on the design, covering the parts of the egg that are to remain the light color. Return the egg to the same dyebath, this time until a medium depth of color is achieved. It may be rinsed in clean water again to soften the second shade of color. Wax on the final part of the design to cover those parts of the shell that are to remain the medium shade and finally dye the egg again in the same dyebath until it takes on the deepest tone of the color. Pat dry, remove the wax and you will have a three-toned egg with white accents.

An orange wash allows you to dye over bright or deep colors by fading out green, blue, red and brown from parts of the shell that are to be colored differently. It makes it possible to combine different bright or deep colors on one egg in their true shades that would otherwise discolor one another. For instance, bright red poppies can be dyed over green leaves. Simply keep an extra cup of orange dye on hand. Dye the egg as per regular dyeing instructions until a deep shade has been applied that you wish to dye over. Pat the egg dry, apply the next portion of the design in wax and place the egg in the orange dye to neutralize the unprotected parts of the underlying bright shade. The egg will now take another bright shade, in those parts that have been washed out, without discoloration of either color.

TYPES OF WAX

There are three different kinds of wax that can be used in egg decorating, each with its own individual properties. Beeswax is the best wax to use for wax-resist methods. It has a higher melting point than either paraffin or crayon wax, which means it dries more quickly after it is applied to the eggshell. It also provides smooth, even coverage, is the least likely to smear and resists dye better than the other two. It is also more expensive. Beeswax can be purchased in blocks or disks at craft shops, or as candles in candle or variety shops, but the least expensive form is the little cakes found in fabric shops used to wax straight pins. Only a tiny bit is used for each egg, so a little goes a long way, and as long as you use pure beeswax, regardless of the form in which you purchased it, you will get the same results.

While both paraffin and wax crayons can be used for batik they are better suited to other methods. Paraffin (candle wax) can also be used for wax-dripping or wax-scratching. It is available at supermarkets in inexpensive colorless blocks or as candles in a range of shapes and sizes in almost any color imaginable. It is a petroleum by-product so it is flammable. Melt small amounts of paraffin in a small, clean tin can (such as a tuna can). Set it in a metal saucepan with an inch or so of water. Slowly bring the water to a boil. Colored crayons are wonderful for wax-dripping and for coloring other types of wax. They are inexpensive, available nearly anywhere, and are found in dozens of colors.

FREE-FORM BATIK

This is the simplest batik method. It is easy enough for young children but adult supervision is necessary because of the use of a burning candle. The results are striking free-form splashes of white or light colors against a colored background. A single dye bath produces eye-catching results, while multiple dyeings create explosions of color.

This is a fine method for eggs that are to be eaten. Hard-boil the eggs first and use cold-water, food-safe dyes only.

1. Mix dye according to package directions or recipe.

2. Light candle, hold sideways over egg and allow wax to drip onto the surface. Hold the egg still, and drop small dots of wax to make dots or circles, or turn the egg quickly as the wax drops fall to form streaks. Be careful to avoid touching the flame or the hot wax.

3. Let the wax cool for a few minutes then gently lower the egg into the dye. If using more than one shade, remember to dye the lightest color first. When the egg reaches the desired color, remove it. Allow to air dry on the egg stand, or pat dry with a soft cloth. When dry, it is either finished, or ready for more wax drops and another dye bath, as you wish.

4. When all coats of dye are dry, remove the wax. One way is to hold the egg up to the candle flame, heating one patch of wax at a time and rubbing it clean with a paper towel or soft cloth. Remove the wax from several eggs at once by heating them in a very low (180°F) oven for about 15 minutes. Use a multiple egg stand, leave the oven door ajar, if possible, and keep an eye on them as they heat. As soon as they begin to look wet, the wax is warm enough to rub off. This last step is best left for adults.

5. If raw eggs are used, blow them out after the wax is removed.

6. Apply the finish of your choice to hollow eggs, or vegetable oil to cooked eggs, if desired. See about finishes on pages 9–10.

To make, gather:

Clean, white eggs, raw or hard-boiled

Candle and lighter or match

One or more shades of dye

White vinegar

Cup or container for each dye shade

Tablespoon or wire egg holder

Egg stand

Finish, if desired

BATIK TEARDROP EGGS

Teardrop eggs are simple yet striking; they are also the center of legend. As the tale goes, Jesus was seized by the Roman Emperor Pontius Pilate and condemned to die upon the cross. His mother, Mary, determined to go and plead for the life of her son. She prepared some eggs as an offering to the emperor, but as she worked her tears overcame her and splashed down upon the eggs, leaving brilliant marks wherever they landed. Mary gathered these miraculous eggs into her apron and went to face Pilate. As she fell to her knees, begging in sorrow and grief, the eggs rolled from her apron, across the floor and continued until they had gone out all over the world.

Children are fascinated by the technique for making these eggs. In fact, those as young as ten can get remarkable results. By first applying the wax and then dyeing one bright shade, a striking white design on a colorful background emerges. Or dye the egg a light shade before applying the wax teardrops, then dip in a deeper shade, creating a light design with a dark background. It is most effective to choose colors that will have sharp contrast.

This method requires more time and attention than free-form, but you will very likely wish to preserve them as keepsakes.

To make, gather:

Clean, white eggs, raw or hard-boiled

Beeswax and container for melting (some people prefer mixing paraffin and beeswax 50/50)

Pin-head stylus (see below) or several in different sizes

Rubber bands and pencil to mark design on egg, if desired

Dye and cup for each shade

White vinegar

Tablespoon or wire egg holder

Egg stand

Finish

1. Mix dye according to package directions or recipe.

2. If desired, draw in guidelines using pencil and rubber band.

3. Heat beeswax in container over candle flame. As it heats, it should scorch and turn black. If not, or if you prefer to melt the wax over boiling water, add a small bit of crayon to color the wax. This makes it easier to see it on the egg.

4. Make a pin-head stylus by pushing the sharp end of a straight pin into a pencil eraser. By using pins with different size heads, you can create "tears," dots, and other marks in varying widths.

5. Dip the head of the stylus into hot wax and quickly touch it to the egg. A single touch makes a dot. "Tears," commas, and other marks are formed by making a dot then quickly and smoothly drawing the pin across the egg's surface.

6. Dye the egg. Let each shade dry before applying the next set of wax designs. The egg may be allowed to air dry or gently patted with a soft, dry cloth.

7. Remove wax either by heating the egg over a candle flame or by warming in a low oven. (See page 17, step #4.)

8. If raw eggs are used, blow out after wax is removed.

9. Apply the finish of your choice to hollow eggs, or add a few drops of vegetable oil to cooked eggs.

PYSANKY

Pysanky, the intricate, elaborate, astonishingly beautiful art of Ukrainian egg decoration is to Easter what fireworks are to the Fourth of July. It is every bit as spectacular and certainly longer lasting!

In the Ukraine and surrounding areas, this folk art was a well-established practice even before the advent of Christianity and its influences. It is from this highly specialized and stylized form of egg decorating that so many of the traditional symbols evolved. Year after year, ever more detailed and beautiful pysanky designs are turned out by some truly gifted artists.

There are many Ukrainian beliefs surrounding pysanky. For centuries the eggs were thought to be imbued with supernatural powers, such as the belief that they could cure blood poisoning merely by having the sick person touch one. Often they were inscribed with fertility symbols, such as hens, roosters, or oak leaves, and offered as gifts to those wishing to conceive children. A basket of pysanky, kept in the house, was insurance against fire, crop failure, and evil spirits.

One old legend has it that pysanky alone is the key to the fate of the world. An evil monster awaits the end of the practice of pysanky. He is chained, somewhere, to a massive cliff, surrounded by demons who apprise him of the status of the art with a count of how many eggs are decorated every year. In years where the numbers dwindle, the chains of the beast loosen and he strains against them, ready to destroy the world and all that is in it. But in years when the number of eggs decorated increases, his chains tighten and he is subdued. We are safe as long as there are those with the faith, patience, and creativity to practice pysanky but should the practice end, the monster will be set free, and we will be at his mercy.

Whether practiced for its delicate beauty or to save the world, pysanky is an art form well worth the effort of mastering. Though the process is basically the same as for other forms of batik, it requires fine motor skills and much patience. Some of the designs take hours or days, through several

PIN-HEAD STYLUS METHOD:

To make a pin-head stylus, see page 18, step #4. The technique used depends on the form of beeswax you are using. You can melt the wax first and dip the pin-head into it, thereby picking up a tiny bit of wax. By quickly touching this to the egg before it dries you can apply it to the shell. Another method is to hold the pin in a candle flame for a few seconds and then touch to the beeswax. The hot pin-head will melt a tiny bit of wax which sticks to it. Quickly apply the wax to the eggshell. A third technique is to light a beeswax candle and use the pin-head tip to pick up melted wax as it pools at the foot of the flame. All of these methods are fine for dots and teardrops, and if necessary can be adapted, through practice and patience, to create extended lines. But for consistent, clean lines and clear drawings, you need a kistka.

applications of wax and dye, to complete. All this work has earned the eggs the nickname of "tortured eggs," referring to the painstaking, time-consuming process of decoration. Properly handled and stored, they can last indefinitely, with many in private collections being passed from one generation to the next.

To make, gather:

Clean, raw egg

Dyes and containers for each color

Beeswax

Candle and lighter or match

Kistka or stylus (see page 21); one or several of varying sizes

Pencil and rubber bands for marking guidelines

Clean, soft cloth or paper towels

Finish

Egg stand

1. Decide on your design. Sketch it out on paper the same size as it will appear on the egg. This will give you an idea of how it will fit and what may need to be modified. And it will be good practice for your hands, especially with intricate patterns.

2. If desired, lightly pencil any guidelines onto the egg. Bear in mind that they will not be removed, so they should be as unobtrusive as possible. A faint line of colored pencil, a shade lighter than the color to be dyed over it, virtually disappears when the egg is dyed.

3. Using the guidelines, carefully draw and/or fill in the parts of the design that are to remain white. To do this, you dip in wax either a pin-head stylus, a kistka, or a combination of the two depending on the design. See the following instructions in using the pin-head stylus and the kistka.

4. Dye the egg the first (lightest) shade. When the desired color is reached, usually after only a few minutes for light shades, remove the egg and pat (not rub) or air dry.

5. Leaving the previous wax on the egg, add more wax to cover those parts of the egg that are to remain the color of the first dyebath.

6. Dye the egg the next darkest shade and continue the process of waxing and dyeing until the design is complete. When finished, remove all the wax, either by holding the egg up to a flame or by setting in a warm oven (see page 17, step #4). Whenever using the candle method to melt wax, be certain not to hold the egg directly over the candle smoke or the dye can scorch, ruining all your hard work and creative effort.

7. Blow the egg and apply finish.

KISTKA METHOD

There are easier things to master than drawing on an egg. The shape, weight, and fragility all make for some clumsiness on the part of the apprentice egg artist. The first order of business is to get comfortable. Some of the designs take a long time to complete, and an unnatural or strained position makes a tragic egg accident all the more likely. Sit at a table and work with your arms supported on it. It's a good idea to hold the egg over a folded towel with one hand and to hold the kistka with the other.

The kistka is the traditional instrument of Ukrainian pysanky. They are available commercially through Ukrainian gift shops (see Appendix for mail-order information) and include several sizes and types. The metal tip is heated by holding it to a candle. When hot, dip it in beeswax to collect the melted wax in the funnel. The wax is then applied to the egg through the hole in the tip. The process is repeated time after time. Trial and error will show you just how much is enough, as too much will cause the wax to overflow or drip. Overheating the head will cause the same problems. The heat of the flame will also cause the beeswax to turn black, but this is not a problem. In fact, this is preferable to the natural state of beeswax, which is nearly transparent, as the blackened wax is much easier to see on the egg.

There are electric kistkas available that speed things up because the tip is kept hot without having to repeatedly hold it in the flame. Some people find that the electric kistka makes it easier to draw even lines. The gentle heating of an electric kistka prevents discoloration, but you can pre-color the wax by either scorching over a candle flame (use an old tin can) or by adding a small bit of crayon to melted wax. Let the pre-colored wax cool before using.

Draw by holding the kistka perpendicular to the surface of the egg. If you are using different sized tips, it is recommended to start with the fine or medium tip for each stage of the design, using the heaviest tip last. The wax should flow smoothly from the tip; when it stops, reheat over the candle flame, add more wax, and continue working. (With an electric kistka you need only add more wax and continue.)

The variations for pysanky designs are endless. There are helpful books and kits available (see Appendix).

A HOMEMADE KISTKA

You can make your own kistka just as eastern European artisans have for hundreds of years. Though perhaps somewhat crude looking, it has certainly proven to be a serviceable instrument.

You will need:

A straight piece of green (fresh) stick about six inches long and as thick as a comfortable pen. It is worthwhile to cut a fresh stick because dry wood becomes kindling as soon as it meets the candle flame.

A piece of metal foil about ½ by ¾ inch. Brass shim stock (available through automotive supply stores) works well, as will other re-cycled bits of found metal.

Pocketknife, or other small sharp blade

Needle

Fine wire, about 10 inches in length

1. Use the needle as a form and wrap the metal foil tightly around it to make a narrow funnel about ½ inch long. Remove needle.

2. Carefully make two ¼-inch long cuts into one end of the stick, bringing them together at the ends to form a narrow "V."

3. Push the funnel snugly into the "V" so that about ⅛ inch is above the stick, and the rest is beneath.

4. Wrap the wire around the funnel and stick several times in a figure eight, and twist the ends together.

EASY PYSANKY

For those just beginning to experiment with wax-resist dyeing, the elaborate designs of traditional pysanky may seem a bit overwhelming. Try a scaled-down version of the craft first to get you started. But beware, you may get hooked! Easy Pysanky is suitable for kids of all ages because you will be making a simple light-and-dark design. Children can make whatever logos, patterns, objects, or designs they like on the dyed eggs. A friend's son made a collection of sports company logos on his eggs!

To make, gather:

The same materials as for pysanky (see page 20)

1. Follow the instructions as for pysanky, but simplify the design. It's amazing how striking a few swirls or simple geometric patterns look on the finished eggs. Apply designs in wax to either a white egg or an egg dyed a light shade. Then dip in a dark dye and remove wax. This process is so quick and easy, but yields such pleasing results that it makes the perfect primer for one about to try the more formal version of pysanky.

CHEAT BATIK

Another type of wax-resist dyeing might well be regarded as "cheating" because it is so easy. Instead of using instruments and melted wax, all you need are color crayons. This method is great for even the youngest kids. It is fine for use on cooked eggs as long as only food-safe dyes are used.

To make, gather:

Clean, white eggs, raw or hard-boiled
White or colored crayons
Dye and cup for each color
Vinegar
Rubber band or masking tape for lines
Finish

1. Mix dye according to package directions or recipe. Add 1 to 2 teaspoons vinegar per cup.

2. Use rubber band or masking tape to draw any guidelines your design may need.

3. Using a *white* crayon, draw in any parts of your design that are to be white.

4. Dye the egg.

5. If desired, color in other areas and re-dye.

6. Allow the egg to dry and finish, if desired.

Variation: Substitute colored crayons in step three and draw on your entire design, using different colors wherever you like. Keep in mind that heavy lines show up best after dyeing.

WAX RELIEF

A totally different approach to decorating eggs with wax is the wax-relief method. Unlike wax-resist, where the wax is removed from the egg after decorating, here the wax **is** the decoration.

Wax relief creates a raised pattern which may be of a single color on a white egg, or one or more colors on a pre-dyed egg. It is easy for children to master, but does require fine motor skills. Since a little or a lot of effort can go into these eggs, they may be suitable for eggs to be eaten or for keepsake eggs. But, as always, if the eggs are to be eaten, use only food-safe colorings.

1. Be sure eggs are perfectly dry before applying wax.

2. Color plain beeswax by melting with a tiny bit of color crayon over the candle flame in a throw-away tin or foil-lined cup. Let harden and remove from tin.

3. Work a small ball of wax, about one inch around, between your fingers, warming occasionally over the candle flame to keep it pliable. Flatten the wax between two pieces of foil.

4. Remove the top piece of foil. Use the knife or razor blade to cut shapes from the colored beeswax. Simple shapes, such as triangles, squares, leaves, clo-

verleafs, wavy ribbons, etc. can be arranged onto the egg in an endless array of pleasing patterns.

5. Pick up each piece with the tweezers, and hold for an instant near the candle flame with the back side of the piece nearest the heat. Quickly place the wax piece, melted side down, in place on the egg. Press lightly with a fingertip to secure in place.

To make, gather:

Clean eggs, white or pre-dyed, blown or hard-boiled

Colored beeswax

Small sharp knife or single-edged razor blade

Tweezers

Candle

EMBOSSED TEARDROP EGGS

This is another type of wax relief, using the same techniques as for batik teardrop eggs. Here, too, simple dots, commas, and teardrops can be combined for a limitless variety of patterns. You may use one color of beeswax or several, using a white egg, brown egg, or dyed egg. This method is easy enough for school-age children, yet varied and challenging enough for adults. If food-safe dyes are used, it can be applied to edible eggs as well as those destined to become family heirlooms.

1. Be sure eggs are thoroughly dry before applying wax.

2. Gently melt beeswax in tin over candle flame. If it is not already colored, add the color of your choice by breaking off a tiny bit of crayon and stirring into melted wax with a toothpick.

3. Dip pin-head stylus into melted wax, and quickly touch it to the egg shell. Remember that a single touch makes a dot, while light strokes create teardrop shapes. Unlike in batik teardrop eggs, here the designs must be worked freehand, as any penciled in guidelines would show.

To make, gather:

Clean eggs, white, brown, or pre-dyed, blown or hard-boiled

Colored beeswax

Pin-head stylus, one or several sizes

Melting tin

Candle

WAX DRIPPING

Combine bright colors, eager kids, and an excuse to decorate, and you are bound to get brilliant results! Wax dripping is another easy way to produce striking, colorful eggs that will really stand out. "Dropped-wax eggs," as the results are known, will add sparkle to any egg hunt. Because a burning candle is used, adult supervision is necessary.

To make, gather:

Hard-boiled eggs, plain or pre-dyed

3 or 4 different colored crayons in contrasting shades

Candle

Egg stand

Wax paper, paper towel, or plastic to protect work area

1. Let egg rest in egg stand right next to lit candle. Heat the tip of the crayon near (not in) the candle flame. Don't put the crayon directly in the flame as the wax will scorch and form black streaks.

Use long crayons, or hold shorter ones with tweezers or an alligator clip to keep your fingers as far from the flame as possible.

2. As the crayon heats, it will turn glossy and look wet. Just as a droplet of hot wax begins to drip from the crayon, move it over the egg and let the wax drip down onto the surface. You can let the different colored drops dribble down the sides of the egg to create a colorful, raised, free-form pattern, or you can try to control the path of the wax droplets by holding the egg in one hand and quickly turning it just as the droplets land.

3. The wax cools and dries very quickly, and any spots you don't like can be flicked off with a fingernail.

SCRATCHED WAX EGGS

This technique is similar to wax carving (see page 25), in that a coat of wax serves as the background to a design that is carved through it. The difference here is that the wax coating is crayon wax that is simply rubbed onto the eggshell. Scratched wax eggs are great fun for kids; the bright colors of the finished design being a delightful surprise even to the artist. It is best used on hard-boiled eggs, because raw or hollow eggs may not withstand the pressure of having crayons firmly rubbed against them. Eggs decorated in this way are fine for eating. Note: this is basically the same procedure as filling a piece of drawing paper with bright colors, covering it all with heavy black crayon, then scratching out a design or a picture.

To make, gather:

Hard-boiled eggs at room temperature. Those fresh from the refrigerator or still hot from the pan will not take crayon wax well.

Several different shades of crayon

Black crayon

One or more scratching tools, such as a nail, needle, or craft knife

1. Color the entire surface of the egg with patches of various colors. Go over the entire egg in patterns, stripes, or random patches so that it is completely covered. Bright or pastel colors will give the best results.

2. Color over everything with a solid layer of black crayon.

3. Using one or more scratching tools, etch out a design on the surface of the egg. The different colors hiding beneath the black make every pattern unique.

CARVED WAX EGGS

Here is a sort of "reverse-pysanky." The process is simple and can produce beautiful, intricate results. Older children who have developed fine motor skills and a fair amount of tolerance for careful work will find it challenging and rewarding.

Carved wax eggs are safe to eat after the waxed shell has been peeled away, as long as any dyes used are edible.

1. Slowly melt wax by placing it in a container and setting it in a pan with an inch or two of simmering water. With a wooden spoon or stick, stir in a small bit of crayon to add color. Stir until smooth and evenly colored.

2. Submerge the egg in the melted wax. Remove and wait a few minutes for the wax to cool and harden.

3. When the wax is dry, carve a design by using a single-edged razor blade or an Exacto knife to cut away the wax to reveal the surface of the egg. A needle or toothpick is sometimes helpful in prying loose tiny bits of wax. If using a white egg, the results will be a white design carved out of coating of colored wax. (A pre-dyed egg results in a colored pattern.)

To make, gather:

Clean, dry eggs, white or pre-dyed, raw or hard-boiled

Melted, colored wax, equal parts paraffin and beeswax will produce the best results. You will need about ½ cup wax, or enough to completely immerse the egg.

Small throw-away containers, just large enough to dunk and completely cover each egg. A soup can works well.

Craft knife, single-edged razor blade, or other sharp tool for scratching away wax.

WORKING WITH WAX

BLEACHED BATIK

Here is an unusual twist to the art of egg batik. Instead of the wax preventing certain areas of the egg from taking dye, here wax is used to preserve the dye color while the rest of the egg is chemically bleached. The result is a colored design, either free-form or patterned, over a bleached, grainy-looking background. Batik one egg and bleach another using the same pattern to create a set where one egg is the exact negative of the other.

The bleaching process makes these eggs unsuitable for eating and also makes adult supervision a must.

To make, gather:

Clean, raw eggs, dyed in a dark or bright shade.

Wax to make the design. You can use a dripping wax candle or beeswax and a stylus for a more formal design.

Bleaching ingredients:

1 tablespoon chloride bleach to 1 cup water or 1 tablespoon baking soda in 1 cup cool water or 1 tablespoon citric acid crystals which have been dissolved in ¼ cup hot water with enough cool water added to make 1 cup.

Glass container

Egg stand

1. Drip or draw design onto dyed egg and wait a few minutes for the wax to cool.

2. Gently lower the egg into the bleaching solution. The dye may take as little as two minutes or more than ten to bleach from the unprotected parts of the eggshell.

3. Remove the egg and rinse well. Let dry on egg stand.

4. Remove wax (see page 17, step #4).

5. Finish as desired.

BLOCK DYEING

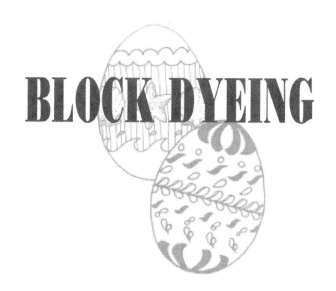

As wonderful and versatile as it is, wax-resist dyeing is but one kind of resist dyeing. There are many others. While the materials for batik are usually readily available and the carefully planned results rewarding, other types of resist dyeing offer the challenges of gathering unusual materials and producing often surprising results.

LEAF BLOCKING

Leaf blocking is a very old method of egg decorating that is still popular in many places today. In Austria delicate leaf-decorated eggs are traditional. It is common practice for children to gather small leaves, ferns, or wildflowers to lend their distinctive silhouettes to decorated eggs. There are many variations; herbs, grasses, or fabric or lace cutouts can all be used. Natural, edible dyes are the preferred.

Older children will find the endless possibilities an exciting challenge and enjoy gathering materials as much as, or more than, putting them to use. Leaf-decorated eggs traditionally all were decorated with natural dyes. See the chapter on Dyes and Dyeing for suggestions on gathering and using food-safe natural dyes.

To make, gather:

Clean, white eggs, raw or hard-boiled

(Note: When using natural dyes, the eggs may be cooked and dyed in the same step.)

Dyeing materials according to the dye method of your choice

Small leaves (the more finely divided the foliage, the more delicate the design the leaf will make), flowers, ferns, grasses, pieces of lace or fabric cut into interesting shapes

Very fine thread, or sections of fine gauze or old nylon stocking, about six inches square or self adhesive wall-repair fabric (available in hardware stores), which has the advantage of being both tacky and flexible.

Salad oil or lightly beaten egg white or sodium silicate solution (from craft shop)

1. Rinse collected leaves or flowers in cool water and blot dry with paper towels.

2. Dip each leaf, etc., in oil, egg white, or sodium silicate solution and shake off excess.

3. Carefully place each piece on the egg. If more than one is used per egg, arrange in a pleasing design. Take care not to smear the oil (or other solution) on the eggshell, as it may prevent the dye from taking. Once the leaf is placed, it should not be moved unless the egg is cleaned and you start over.

4. Use the thread, gauze, nylon, or fabric to firmly bind the pieces to the egg. The more tightly they are secured, the less likely the dye is to seep beneath and mar the design.

5. Dye with the method of your choice. A medium-to-dark or bright shade will produce the most contrast with the white imprint of the leaf. Fine thread or stocking may leave no distinguishable markings on the egg, but gauze and wall-repair tape will add a faint grid-like pattern.

6. Allow the egg to dry completely before removing the leaf or other objects, then finish with the method of your choice.

Variation: Try using noncolor-fast fabric cut-outs or crepe paper. The dye will leach from them onto the surface of the egg. You can use these cut-outs with a contrasting shade of dye or alone in a warm water solution.

STICKER BLOCKING

Here's one for the littlest egg decorators. Even though this method is very easy to do, the results are distinctive and the variety of patterns limitless. The eggs may be dyed once to create a white design against a colored background, pre-dyed to turn out a pastel design against a dark background, or dyed several times to produce different colored designs. If food-safe dyes are used, sticker blocking is a great way to decorate cooked eggs.

1. Prepare dye according to package directions or recipe.

2. Arrange stars, circles, strips, and other shapes on the surface of the egg. If you will be dyeing more than one color, be sure to leave some empty areas to place stickers for the next dye bath.

3. Dye the egg. Pat dry or let dry on egg stand.

4. Repeat steps 2 and 3 as desired.

5. Remove all stickers and apply finish.

Variation: After the egg has dried, apply some of the same shape stickers used to block the dye and leave on the egg.

To make, gather:

Clean eggs, raw or hard-boiled, white or pre-dyed a light shade

Dyeing materials

Gummed stars, paper-reinforcement rings, shapes cut from gummed labels, strips of masking tape, or gummed labels.

Egg stand

Finish

RUBBER BAND EGGS

Create bold expressions of color that seem to defy the "laws" of egg dyeing by using rubber bands. Half the fun is in making patterns from the rubber bands, but a simple, sly secret makes this technique all the more intriguing. These eggs are sure to get rave reviews at the Easter-egg hunt, just remember to use only edible dyes if they are to be eaten.

1. Prepare dye according to package directions or recipe.

2. Arrange rubber bands over the areas of the egg you wish to remain white (or pre-dyed color).

3. Dye egg. You may wish to dye only one color creating a white (or light) pattern against a dark background or several shades.

The trick: Remembering that you can only normally dye dark colors over light, and that each coat of dye is

affected by the one before it, some of the color combinations you can create with rubber band eggs will seem like a real puzzle. Use the wire egg holder to hold the egg in the dye only part way, so that the dye only covers one end of the egg. When the egg is dry, reverse the process. For details, see page 9.

4. Repeat steps 2 and 3 until you get the design you want.

5. Remove all rubber bands and apply the finish of your choice.

To make, gather:

Clean eggs—raw or hard-boiled, white or pre-dyed.

Rubber bands of assorted widths, long enough to fit snugly around the egg.

Dyeing materials

Wire egg holder (as from supermarket kits)

Egg stand

Finish of your choice

TIE-DYED EGGS

Dramatically different, tie-dyed eggs are a mystery, even to their creator, until the moment they are unwrapped. They can be made by young children, and the suspense and bright colors make them fun for older kids as well. By using food coloring, you can tie-dye cooked eggs to be eaten.

To make, gather:

Clean, white eggs, raw or hard-boiled

Dye or food coloring

A six-inch square of lightweight cotton cloth

Two rubber bands or pieces of string for each egg (to secure cloth)

1. Prepare dye according to package directions or recipe.

2. Wrap the egg in cloth and fasten against each end of the egg with a rubber band.

3. Immerse the wrapped egg in the dye, being certain to thoroughly wet the cloth.

4. Let dry overnight, then unwrap and enjoy.

RAINBOW EGGS

Like tie-dyed eggs, the results are a mystery until they are unveiled. These eggs are easy enough for small children, yet have that mysterious appeal that even adults enjoy. Food coloring makes them safe to eat.

To make, gather:

Clean, white, hard-boiled eggs

Eyedropper (to apply coloring)

Food coloring (or edible egg dyes) in two or three bright, contrasting colors

A six-inch square of lightweight cotton cloth.

White vinegar

1. Dilute food coloring or mix dye in a tablespoon of water. It will be much more concentrated than regular dye. Add a few drops of vinegar.

2. Wet the cloth and wring out until it is only slightly damp. Wrap it around the egg.

3. Fill the eye-dropper with one color and release drops onto the cloth, all around the egg. Rinse the dropper and repeat with the other two colors.

4. Holding the cloth at each end, give a twist to run the colors together. This creates the rainbow effect.

5. Let dry a few minutes, then remove the cloth, and behold.

ETCHING & SCRATCHING

 ctually, we have already discussed one type of etching under the heading "Bleach Batik", in which a corrosive bath was used to strip color from dyed eggshell. Another type of etching uses a stronger solution of bleach to etch out a design. Still another technique for removing dye in order to fashion a design is to simply scratch it from the egg with a sharp tool. With any of these methods, a deep shade of dye should be used to contrast with the exposed shell.

Due to the use of chemicals and sharp instruments, these methods are not recommended for children.

ETCHING

Egg etching is a simple technique, nonetheless, extreme care must be taken when handling the acid used to eat away the dye. The results can be as simple or as ornate as you choose.

To make, gather:

Clean, blown eggs, pre-dyed a dark shade

Small bottle of 3% hydrochloric acid (available in drugstores) or household bleach diluted 50/50 with water

Nib pen or toothpick

1. Work out a design on paper in the same size as it will be on the egg. The design can be drawn onto the egg in pencil, since the acid will remove the pencil marks on contact.

2. Dip pen nib or end of toothpick into the acid, and draw the design onto the egg, one small portion at a time. The acid will eventually ruin the metal tip of a pen so you may opt for a toothpick. You will have to dip a toothpick in the acid much more frequently than a pen, however, which makes the process slower. The acid will instantly bleach away any color wherever it touches the dyed egg, so steady hands are a must. Finished eggs will boast a delicate, white pattern against a dark background.

3. Rinse thoroughly in cold water, blot dry, and add a finish. Note: Any drips onto the egg will bleach and ruin the pattern. Careful work should avoid any drips. Have an absorbant cloth handy just in case.

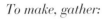

SCRATCHING

Here is another old, simple technique, that, like etching, can produce astonishingly intricate results. The only limits are the inspiration, skill, and steadiness of the artist. By the 1700s scratching was popular among the Pennsylvania Dutch, with whom birds and flowers were common themes.

1. Plan your design and sketch it out on paper. It can be penciled onto the egg as the lines will be scratched off as the design is scratched on.

2. Using the sharpest point of your tool, gently and carefully scratch the dye from the shell along the pattern lines. This is a time-consuming method that requires patience and a steady hand, but the unique showpiece eggs you create will prove it to be time well spent.

To make, gather:

Clean, dry, pre-dyed eggs, raw or hard-boiled.

(Note: Holding and scratching the egg exerts a good deal of force against the shell. Hard-boiled eggs stand up to the pressure better than raw, while hollow eggs are the most fragile. It is best to blow the eggs out after scratch decorating.)

A single-edged razor, Exacto knife, pen-knife, or other sharp scratching tool

CUSTOM COLORING

Even though eggs and dye seem to go hand-in-hand for many of us, there are scores of other ways to bring color into the life of plain, white eggs. Sponging and marbleizing are unique ways to decorate eggs using paint, but no paintbrush. Sparkling, swirling, hypnotic waves of color create fascinating eggworks.

SPONGING

Nothing could be simpler. In less than a minute you can create sparkling, dappled eggs in bright, cheerful colors. Sponging is fine fun for kids, but due to the use of paints, not recommended for eggs that are to be eaten.

To make, gather:

Clean white eggs, whole or blown

Nontoxic, liquid acrylic paints

Sponge

Egg stand

1. Dip a corner section of the sponge in the paint and smooth it over the sponge with a finger or toothpick so that a one- or two-inch square section is evenly coated. Blot excesses on a paper towel.

2. Holding the egg between the thumb and index finger of one hand, dab with the sponge all around except where your fingers contact it. Set on egg stand to dry for a few minutes.

3. When the paint is dry enough to handle without smearing, hold onto the middle of the egg and dab the ends. Let dry.

4. Finish as desired.

MARBLING

Marbling is an ancient method of paper and fabric decorating. Practiced in Japan, China, and Persia since antiquity, the process remains much the same. The craft reached Europe late in the 18th century and took on new twists with each country that adopted it along the way.

Until recently, examples of this fascinating craft were few: the inside covers of old books being the most common. But marbling is experiencing a revival. Although there are formal patterns, no two marbled pieces look exactly alike. Bright, contrasting colors, subtle blends of pastel shades, delicate swirls, bold splashes, waves and curls — all radiate from the page. Or egg.

There are two substantial challenges to marbling eggs versus fabric or paper. Untreated eggshell will not accept paints from the marbling bath reliably, and eggs aren't flat. Whereas a piece of fabric or paper is quickly laid out flat over the bath, an egg calls for special handling. Every egg is a surprise and you are sure to find the process, as well as the eggs it produces, fun, intriguing, and appealing.

Kids love marbling, especially manipulating the paints into interesting patterns. The preparation involved requires adult participation, but the decorating process is for kids of all ages.

To make, gather:

Clean, white eggs, raw or blown

Alum crystals (available in supermarkets)

Acrylic paints in four (or more) colors

Note: Inexpensive paints work as well as costly brands, but always use paints from the same manufacturer in the same bath. Differences in weight and manufacturing make different brands incompatible in a marbling bath.

Carrageenan bath (prepared 12 to 14 hours in advance), see below.

Distilled water or oxgall (from art stores) to thin paints

Bath container — inexpensive paint roller trays work well

Nonmetal mixing bucket

Rubber gloves, if desired

Tools to manipulate paints, such as eye-droppers, hair picks, bamboo skewers, old toothbrush, special marbling combs

1. The day before marbling prepare the carrageenan bath according to package directions. It must have at least 12 to 14 hours to set before it is ready to use. (When you are done, it can be stored in the refrigerator for up to two weeks and reused as often as you like during that time.)

There are two types of carrageenan sold for marbling, one type re- quires heating and one is prepared in a blender.

2. Mix 2 tablespoons of alum crystals in a quart of warm water until all the crystals are dissolved. Pour into a container deep enough to completely cover several eggs and place the eggs into the solution to soak. Eggs that are not pretreated will not accept the paint from the marbling bath. Allow the eggs to soak several minutes, then remove them to an egg rack to drip-dry. DO NOT RINSE.

3. Pour the carrageenan bath into the marbling tray. You may wish to skim off any bubbles.

4. Thin paints with a little distilled water a few drops at a time, or a few drops of oxgall. This is the most unpredictable part of marbling. Paints that are not thinned well enough, sink to the bottom of the bath and will not adhere to the eggs. Those that are thinned too much spread so quickly and thinly across the top of the bath that they are nearly invisible, which is how they will appear on the egg. When paints that are thinned to perfection are dropped onto the bath, they float and slowly spread out into a small circle. It is a good idea to experiment with the thinned paints by using an eyedropper to release a drop of paint into the bath and observe how it floats. Repeat, with a separate eye-dropper for each shade. When you are satisfied with the consistency of the paints, take a few strips of newspaper and skim the test spots from the bath.

5. Now you are ready to create! Put the paints into the bath. This requires a little finesse — even the most perfectly thinned paints will plunk to the bottom if carelessly flung into the bath, or if dropped from too high. It is important to move smoothly and not too quickly when applying the paints. There are several techniques to do this, each creating its own look. Paints may be dropped, from a level just above the bath, with an eye-dropper. Or make a whisk by tying several broom straws together, then dip into the paint and shake or fling it over the bath. This makes a fine spray of speckles. Another technique is to let droplets run off the end of a toothpick into the bath. A simple rule to remember is that the larger the drops, the closer they must be to the bath when they are released lest they sink to the bottom. Continue dropping paint onto the bath until the surface is crowded with splotches of paint.

6. Using whatever tools you have handy (see supply list or make special ones), manipulate the paints to create a pattern. Swirl them together, criss-cross the surface, spatter dots by flicking a little paint from the end of an old toothbrush.

7. The shape of an egg makes it more challenging to marble than a nice, flat sheet of paper. You may have to experiment to find the best approach for you. To transfer the paint onto the egg, you must carefully roll the egg across the surface of the paint pattern. Some people find it easier to submerge the egg and see how the pattern emerges. In either case, it is important to keep a firm grip on the egg with as little finger contact as possible to avoid smudging the paint. By grasping the egg between the thumb and forefinger, you can touch it to the surface of the bath and pick up a circle or oval of paints. Push the egg a little deeper into the bath, and you can color one half of the egg. Let that half dry, then dip the other side for a two-sided decoration. The surface of the egg picks up the paint the instant it comes into contact with it, so the process takes only seconds.

8. Rinse the egg in clear water (keeping your fingers in position so as not to smudge the paints) and place it on a three-point egg stand to dry.

9. When the paint is dry, apply a coat of finish.

10. Skim the paint from the carrageenan bath. Store the bath in clean, plastic jugs in the refrigerator. The thinned paints can be emptied into small glass jars for storage.

LESS FUSS, MORE MESS MARBLING

Though it lacks the history and sophistication of formal marbling, the Less-Fuss method also produces interesting results. While suitable for kids, adult supervision is recommended.

To make, gather:

Clean, white eggs, raw or blown

Throw-away container large enough to dunk an egg, such as an old margarine, cottage cheese, or yogurt container

Can of spray paint

Plastic garbage liners to protect work area

Plastic gloves to protect hands

1. Fill container ¾ full of warm water.

2. Holding the spray paint can a few inches from the surface of the water, spray into it for 4 to 6 seconds.

3. Submerge egg into painted water and remove.

4. Rinse, let dry, and add finish.

SPONGE MARBLING

Marble-like eggs that look as though they were carved of solid stone and polished to a brilliant luster can be faked. Though these eggs look as solid as the real thing, they are actually lightweight, hollow eggshells, cleverly disguised with a bit of paint and lacquer to impersonate stone. Sponge marbling is easy enough for kids to do.

To make, gather:

Clean, white eggs, raw or blown

Acrylic paint in three shades of the same color: dark, medium, and light, and white

Masking tape

Small paint brush

Soft bristled paint, or make-up brush

Sponge

Finish

1. Paint egg with the darkest shade. Let dry.

2. Cut or tear masking tape into irregularly shaped pieces. Arrange on the egg in a random pattern.

3. Thin a medium shade of paint with water until about the consistency of cream.

4. Dip sponge in thinned paint, blot on paper towel, then sponge over entire egg.

5. While first coat is still damp repeat steps 3 and 4 with lighter shade, but sponge on more sparingly than the medium shade. Follow this with a very lightly sponged-on coat of white before the paints dry. Between coats dab with a large, soft-bristled paint brush or old make-up brush to blend and blur the edges of the wet paint.

6. As soon as all three coats of paint have been applied and paint is still somewhat wet, peel off the bits of tape. With a detail-artist paint brush, draw erratic lines of the medium-color paint across the face of the egg to mimic the

natural veins found in genuine marble. Swirl thick and thin lines of white paint to create more veins.

7. While paint is still damp, tap around the edges with soft-bristled paint brush, held vertical to the egg, to soften the edges and veins into a more natural look.

8. When the paint has dried, finish with a coat of clear varnish or fingernail polish. This final step, like polishing of real stone, is what brings out the beauty, and surprising realism of the piece.

Hints: Place the bits of tape so that you can use them as finger contact points while holding onto the egg. This avoids smudging and painted fingers. Also, save money by purchasing only two shades of your chosen color and mixing the third, or lightest shade, by adding a little white paint to the medium shade. Colors that suggest a realistic marble or quartz effect are black/grey, rose/coral, brown/beige, and emerald/green.

PAINTING & PRINTING

You need not be an artist to paint or print superb eggs that will make you look like one. From simple stenciled motifs or whimsical animal images to eggshell portraits, the possibilities of egg painting or printing are inexhaustible.

MEDIUMS

Since there is no end to the possibilities of how an egg can be decorated with paints, there may also seem to be no end to the type of paints you can use. But a handful are preferred. Acrylics are a favorite for painting eggs because they are inexpensive, come in a wide spectrum of vivid colors — most of which are ready to use straight from the tube — and give smooth, even coverage. Clean-up is easy, rinse brushes with warm, soapy water, and sponge off the work area before paints dry. Changes to an acrylic painted egg can be made by carefully wiping away wet paint with a bit of tissue or a damp cotton swab or by dabbing at dried paint with a little paint thinner.

Watercolors are also very popular for their lovely, translucent shades and the soft, fluid effect they create. And they are low-cost and readily available. Clean-up with watercolors is very easy. They are water soluble, which means any moisture, even a damp fingertip, can cause them to bleed. Even dry watercolors will bleed if they get wet. To prevent your masterpiece from literally running away, paint only a portion of the egg at a time and as soon as it is dry, apply a quick coat of clear fingernail polish or other fast-drying finish to protect the fragile colors.

Felt-tip pens provide one of the brightest, easiest ways there is for youngsters to decorate eggs. They are simple to use, come in a rainbow of colors with tips that range from fine line to broad. Many are watercolor, leading to the same problem with bleeding, which can be prevented by applying the finish mentioned above. Many are designed specifically for children, with wide bodies, conical points and nontoxic ink formulas. They can be used freehand, over pencil lines, with stencils, or as a bright accent on dyed eggs.

Fabric writers are a wonderful addition to the egg artist's palette. Inexpensively available in small (1-, 2-, or 4-ounce) tubes, they dispense a line of special paint straight from the container. Poke a small hole through the point of the plastic-pointed bottle, tip the bottle upside down, and squeeze to get a fine, raised line that dries to the touch within minutes. A larger hole causes a fatter line of paint. The paint can be smoothed with the tip of the bottle for flat coverage or piped out in a raised line. The extra dimension adds textural interest to designs, and the explosive color range from pastel to bright, to sparkling metallic, and glitter will really make them shine.

STENCILS

Yes, eggs can be stenciled, but right away the obvious challenge is that curving form. The material used for stenciling on eggs must be flexible and the paint resistant. There are several materials to choose from: masking tape, wax paper, stencil paper, heavy mil plastic, lace, paper lace, doilies, and beeswax. There are even pre-formed, pre-cut commercial egg stencils. To use tape, paper, or plastic, draw the design onto the material then cut out with small, sharp scissors or an Exacto knife. Beeswax, warmed and flattened into a thin sheet, can be drawn on with the tip of a paper clip and the design cut out with an Exacto knife.

The stencil must be firmly attached to the egg so that it doesn't move during stenciling and ruin the appearance of the design. Masking tape is self-sticking, paper, plastic, or fabric must be carefully taped or glued down. Purchased egg-stencils are form fitting. A light spray of nonpermanent spray adhesive will stick the stencil to the eggshell. Another alternative is to brush the back side of the stencil with rubber cement and wait for it to dry, then carefully set the gummed stencil in place on the egg. If you decide to reposition it, it must be re-gummed before it will stick a second time. Either adhesive can be removed by rubbing with a cotton swab that has been dipped in rubber-cement remover. Often, rubber-cement residue can be rubbed off with the fingertips or a pencil eraser. Warmed beeswax can be pressed against the egg, instantly contouring to its form. Peel or melt it off once the stenciling is complete.

To make, gather:

Clean, blown eggs, white or pre-dyed

Stencil material, paper, plastic, etc.

Pencil

Scissors or Exacto knife

Tape, adhesive, or rubber cement

Paint: craft or acrylic types

Paint applicators, such as stencil brushes, sponges, paint brushes, felt-tip markers, old toothbrush, or a piece of clean, soft cloth

Finish

1. Draw stencil design onto stencil material. To translate a design into stencil requires the use of what is known as the stencil bridge. Bridges show up on the finished piece as the gaps between parts of the design, which are caused by the connecting lines on the stencil material. Without these lines the stencil could not hold together. The bridges look the most natural when placed along separation lines in the design, for instance, in between the

petals of a flower. They can easily be introduced into a design by drawing over the existing lines with a heavy-tipped marking pen, and cutting out along the edges of the thickened lines.

2. Cut out the stencil, and affix to the egg.

3. Pour a little paint into an old jar lid or other small container, thin with a little water if necessary.

Dip the end of the paintbrush, sponge, etc. into the paint and dab off any excess onto a paper towel.

4. Holding the paintbrush perpendicular to the eggshell, tap up and down to apply the color. You can

shade or highlight by going over one side of the design more times than the other, or by allowing the first coat to dry and then applying a darker or lighter shade over the top of it.

For a fun and messy alternative try spattering. Dip an old toothbrush into the paint, aim the toothbrush towards the egg, and run your thumb over the bristles so that paint spatters everywhere, hopefully even toward the egg. You can use more than one color if you like. The result is a textured-look stencil design.

5. Remove the stencil, and allow the paint to dry before stenciling more designs or adding a finish.

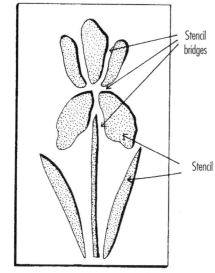

Stencils must be sized to the egg and secured tightly.

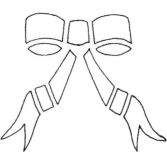

STAINED-GLASS EGGS

These eggs are perfectly suited to watercolors or felt-tip pens (the look can also be captured with batik). The simplest designs resemble the patchwork panes of church windows, while the more elaborate panes may echo late nineteenth-century Art Nouveau. Even though many paints and pens are labeled nontoxic, they are not considered edible and therefore not appropriate for eggs that are to be eaten.

To make, gather:

Clean, white, blown eggs

Paints or felt-tip pens

Black or grey "leading" — fabric writers squeezed straight from the tube leave a raised line, as do stained-glass leading products available at craft stores, or use blackened beeswax.

Egg stand

Finish

1. Draw design on paper or sketch onto egg. For church windows color in irregular patches, leaving a thin gap between each patch and those bordering it.

2. Fill in design in small portions, then let dry to avoid smudging. If using watercolors, brush finish onto each completed section and let it dry before proceeding.

3. When paint and finish are dry, follow any lines or gaps between colored areas with "leading." Don't worry if the lines don't come out perfectly, they can be tidied up with the tip of a toothpick.

An alternative method, commonly used by crafters of leaded stained glass, is to squeeze out straight lines of "leading" from the tube onto plastic wrap that has been placed over lined paper for a guide. Allow the leading to dry, remove any imperfections with the edge of a razor blade or Exacto knife, then peel the leading from the plastic wrap and glue in place on the egg.

HANDPAINTED EGGS

Whether in flowing watercolors or vibrant acrylics, even the simplest handpainted eggs have a special charm all their own. They can be covered with splashes of color or finely detailed portraits. People of all artistic ability enjoy decorating eggs in this straightforward manner.

To make, gather:

Clean, dry, blown eggs, white or pre-dyed a light color

Paints and brushes

Dish of water for rinsing brushes

Pencil

Rubber bands

1. Since paints may spill, be sure to cover the work area.

2. Sketch a design on paper, then, if necessary, lightly pencil onto the egg. Use rubber bands to partition the egg and to guide straight lines (see page 14).

3. Paint one portion of the egg at a time, being careful not to touch wet paint. Let dry on egg stand between each application of paint.

4. When all paint is dry, apply the finish of your choice.

Some suggestions for subjects include traditional Easter themes, such as bunnies, chicks, ducks, and the other symbols described in the section on symbolism. Others to try might include American Indian patterns, designs from wallpaper, gift wrap or greeting cards, quilt or china patterns, vines, ivy and other plants or miniature scenes of everyday life.

TOLE PAINTING

Still popular today, tole painting originated in eighteenth-century New England and with the early Pennsylvania Dutch in America. Floral designs, simple figures, and geometric borders, all perfect for egg decoration, have always been popular themes.

The graceful simplicity of tole painting is perfectly suited to decorating eggs. Colorful designs of bright contrast and complexity can be quickly achieved with swift, single strokes of the paintbrush. These bold, sure strokes convey joy, brimming self-confidence, and a total lack of concern for calculated precision. They appear freeform and effortless. But this self-confidence is born of practice. Although the technique is simple, it absolutely demands a sure and steady hand. Practice is amply rewarded with a natural "feel" for the method and the characteristic flamboyance of those sweeping strokes.

1. Sketch the basic idea of your design on paper before beginning on the egg. Paint over the sketch, if you like for practice.

2. Using any of the following three basic strokes, paint the design you have chosen.

Teardrop: Dip the brush into the paint, getting it fully wet. Ease some of the excess off the brush by pulling it across the rim of the paint container. Touch the still very wet paintbrush to the egg, and allow the paint to pool slightly at the contact point. Draw the wet brush across the egg, gradually lifting it from the surface as you go, until only a thin line remains, then pull the brush away completely. This stroke can be varied by thickness, curved or combined with other strokes for many interesting effects.

Dot or circle: Make dots or circles by touching the wet paintbrush to the egg as above and lifting straight away from the egg's surface. A tightly curled teardrop makes larger circles.

Straight line: Straight lines in tole painting are really elongated, narrowly tapering teardrops. Touch the wet brush to the egg, then rather than allowing the paint to pool, quickly draw the brush along the surface and lift up at the end of the line. Curved lines can be made in the same way and can be combined to outline large ovals or circles.

3. Paint only a portion of the egg at one time to avoid smudges, and let dry on the egg stand in between coats.

4. When all the paint is thoroughly dry, apply the finish of your choice.

TOLE-PAINTED EGGS

Combine bright splashes of color for a floral garland, or paint a single solid color over a pre-dyed or painted egg, such as white over blue in a Wedgewood china mimic.

To make, gather:

Clean, dry, blown eggs, white or pre-dyed

Paints (acrylic or craft types)

Paintbrushes (fine, detail artist's brushes of at least two sizes are recommended)

Egg stand

Finish of your choice

Simple strokes create bold design on tole-painted eggs.

FREEPORT PUBLIC LIBRARY

PRINTED EGGS

From a handful of simple shapes comes an unlimited array of designs, all courtesy of the potato patch. Kids of all ages can create to their hearts content and produce sharp images in attractive patterns. Even hit-and-miss decorators will find this method rewarding.

The secret to good, crisp prints is in the print block. Potatoes make good print blocks for a lot of projects and will work for eggs with a couple of special considerations. Small hands may have difficulty controlling a large spud, especially when using it to decorate an egg that is smaller and infinitely more fragile. When using potatoes as print blocks, select only very fresh, small, firm tubers. A freshly cut spud seeps liquid, a totally unacceptable quality in a printing block. Avoid this problem by preparing potato-print blocks the night before you intend to use them. Carrots, parsnips, turnips, and art-gum erasers make good — even superior — substitutes to traditional potato printers. Any of these can be cut and used immediately, and erasers can be reused indefinitely.

To make, gather:

Clean, dry eggs, raw or blown; white or pre-dyed (whole eggs hold up better to pressure than hollow eggs.)

Print-block material: potatoes, etc.

Paint in one or more colors

A shallow container, such as an old jar lid or foil pan, for each color

Egg stand

Whittle the potato printer to a ½-inch wide point, then carve the point into a simple shape.

1. Prepare print blocks. Remember, if using potatoes to prepare the blocks well ahead of time so that they may dry before being used.

Cut the end from the potato (or other material) and carve down to a narrow end, no more than ½ inch in diameter. This is the printing end of the block. Carefully carve a single shape into this end.

Prepare several blocks of different shapes. A potato will yield two, as will a turnip, while a thick, long carrot or parsnip can be cut into three or four blocks. Either end of an art-gum eraser can be carved, but only one end can be used at time.

2. Dip printing end of the block into paint, and dab once onto paper to blot excess. Press gently but firmly against the egg, being careful not to smudge the print.

3. As with painting, print only a portion of the egg at a time, allowing each area to dry before proceeding.

4. Apply finish if desired.

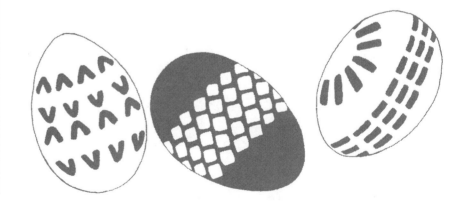

FINGERPAINTED EGGS

There is something about this hands-on, or fingers-on, approach that is downright irresistible. Combine paints, eggs, and kids, and watch the fun. Kids love the feel, the freedom and the splashy, bright colors — and face it, they love a good mess. You can use poster paints, watercolors, or fingerpaints, or make your own, edible version to be used on eggs that are to be eaten.

1. Prepare paints according to package directions and pour each shade into a separate shallow container, such as an old pie tin.

2. Be sure the work area and children's clothing is well-protected.

3. Dip fingers in paints and touch, dab and swirl onto eggs.

4. When finished, allow the eggs to dry on an egg stand (in the refrigerator for cooked eggs).

COW EGGS AND MORE

For a touch of pure whimsy take up your paintbrush or carve out a few footprints to create eggs that no one ever expected the Easter Bunny to deliver.

u Black spots on white eggs for the classic country cow look.

u Create Appaloosa eggs for horsey friends by dyeing one end of the egg and dabbing spots on the other.

u Paint or carve out track prints to run amok across white or dyed eggs.

u Dip the tip of a paintbrush in black paint and jab small irregular dots on white eggs for the dalmatian look or on yellow dyed eggs to capture the look of leopard.

u Paint stripes on white eggs for zebra eggs, or on orange-dyed eggs for the tiger look.

To make, gather:

Clean, white raw or hard-boiled eggs

Fingerpaint (see below)

Plastic garbage liners (to protect work area)

Egg stand

Warm soapy water and soft towels for clean-up

NONTOXIC FINGERPAINTS

1 small envelope gelatin — different flavors produce different colors and enticing aromas, for instance lime-green and cherry-red. You can substitute a packet of unflavored gelatin and a few drops of food coloring.

¼ cup cold water

½ cup cornstarch

¾ cup cold water

2 cups boiling water

1. Add ¼ cup cold water to gelatin and set aside. Mix ¾ cup cold water with cornstarch into a smooth paste. Add paste to boiling water and stir until mixture boils and is clear. Remove from heat and add gelatin. Repeat for each color of paint desired.

NEEDLEWORK EGGS

Trying to picture taking all those tiny stitches through the unlikely fabric of an eggshell? If it sounds impossible, that's very likely because it is — but you can create amazingly real looking needlepoint, cross-stitch or crewel eggs with fabric writers. Forget about how to *make* all those fancy stitches, just study up on what they look like. By using a handful of different color fabric writers you can "stitch" up a collection of beautiful eggs that will definitely get a second look.

To make, gather:

Clean, dry eggs, blown or hard-boiled; white or pre-dyed

Fabric writers in assorted colors

Needlepoint, cross-stitch or crewel pattern, or your own design

Egg stand

Spray finish

1. Pencil design onto egg.

2. Open fabric writer tip by poking with the end of a paper clip or a needle. The larger opening you make, the thicker line. Thicker lines correspond to heavier threads or yarns.

3. Turn writer upside-down, and tap on a piece of paper to fill the writing tip. Practice making a few short, raised lines on paper. These will become the "stitches" on your egg.

4. One small section at a time, fill in the stitches.

5. Let dry on the egg stand overnight, then continue. By doing several eggs at once it won't seem as though you are spending more time waiting for the egg to dry than you are decorating it.

6. After the design is completed and dry, apply a spray finish.

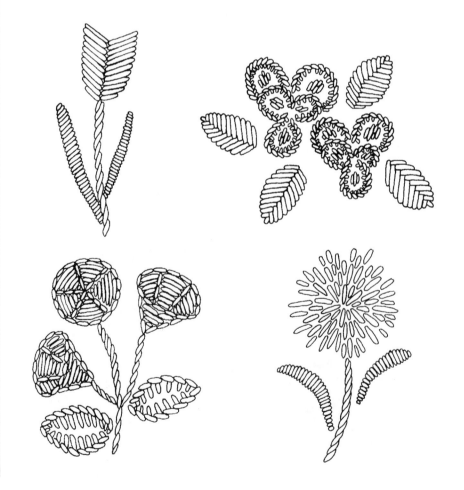

GLUE-ONS

A little glue and what-have-you can make for some engaging Easter eggs. A bit of straw, a scrap of foil, or a handful of beads — along with a little patience and creative spirit, transform a plain egg into a thing of rare beauty. Glue-on projects can be as easy as sticking gold stars on a blue-dyed egg or as involved as creating a gold-relief and rhinestone master-piece to rival the work of Fabergé. There is something here for everyone.

STICKER EGGS

Even tiny tots can get into the act with stickers. Choose small stickers, or gummed stars of different colors for festive eggs. Make your own stickers by gluing the back of tiny paper cutouts or cutting interesting shapes from contact paper.

To make, gather:

Clean, dry hard-boiled eggs, white or pre-dyed

An assortment of stickers

1. Stick 'em on!

GIFT-WRAPPED EGGS

So simple to make, these pretty eggs make the perfect addition to anyone's Easter gift basket.

To make, gather:

Clean eggs, blown or hard-boiled, white or pre-dyed

Satin ribbon, ⅜- to ½-inch wide, 13 to 24 inches per egg

Glue

Accents, such as silk or dried flowers

1. Wrap ribbon around egg lengthwise, and cut a piece long enough to reach around the egg, about 7 inches. Repeat around the widest part of the egg, about 6 inches.

2. Dot glue to wrong side of ribbon and glue in place on the egg, crossing at the front and back gift-wrap style.

3. Glue a bow, flower, or other accent at front cross.

GLITTER EGGS

Sparkling and delightful these easy-to-make eggs are show stoppers. From a random sprinkling to a complex design, glitter decorated eggs get attention.

1. If you would like a formal design, sketch it on paper, then faintly pencil it on the egg.

2. Follow pencil lines that are to be the same color with a line of glue from the glue bottle. Spread glue with a toothpick to cover large areas.

3. Holding the egg over a piece of paper, sprinkle glitter over the glued areas until all are covered. Lightly press the glittered areas with a fingertip and set on egg stand to dry. You may find it easier to do one side, or end, of the egg at a time.

4. Repeat steps 2 and 3 until your design is complete or the entire surface of the egg is covered.

To make, gather:

Clean, dry eggs, raw or hard-boiled, plain or pre-dyed

White glue

Assorted colors of glitter

Toothpick

Paper

Pencil

Egg stand

MOSAIC EGGS

Raid your kitchen cabinets and you are sure to find the stuff that eggworks are made of. Mosaic eggs are unusual, and provide the unique aspect of "feel appeal". What's more anyone can make them.

1. Sketch your design on paper, then lightly onto the egg.

2. For tiny items, apply glue to the eggshell, a small section at a time, then press the pieces into the glue. For larger pieces like macaroni, apply a dot of glue to each piece, then press it lightly onto the shell for a few seconds.

3. Colored pieces, such as dyed rice (see below), can be glued to a plain or pre-dyed egg and allowed to dry for edible egg treats. For the Midas touch, glue macaroni, rice, or other items on the egg, let dry, then spray with a coat of metallic gold spray paint.

To make, gather:

Clean, dry eggs, raw or hard-boiled, plain or pre-dyed

Candy sprinkles, seashells, elbow or alphabet macaroni, plain or colored rice, small dried beans, etc.

Glue

Pencil

Egg stand

COLORED RICE OR MACARONI

1 tablespoon rubbing alcohol

½ teaspoon food coloring

1½ cup uncooked rice or macaroni

Shake together in a sealed plastic bag or any closable plastic or glass container. Scatter a single layer onto a sheet of foil to dry several hours or overnight.

DÉCOUPAGE EGGS

Once described as Poor Man's Art, découpage has flourished, faded and fluctuated as a revived craft. Fine examples can be found everywhere from antique stores to the baby's nursery. Découpage continues to be a wonderfully simple way to dramatically decorate any smooth surface, including Easter eggs. The results depend more on your taste in art than on your ability to create it.

Cut out favorite comic strip characters, gift wrap designs, wallpaper, magazines, garden catalogs, or calendars, to name a few. Heavier stock paper, such as that of greeting cards, won't bend easily enough to follow an egg's rounded shape.

To make, gather:

Clean, dry eggs, raw or hard-boiled, white or pre-dyed

Cut-out pictures

White glue

Artist's paintbrush

Scissors

Cup or small container

1. Trim pictures and arrange on egg, making any adjustments necessary. Snip small darts in the paper anyplace it needs to bend slightly with the curve of the egg.

2. Thin the glue with a few drops of water, and brush onto the wrong side of the picture. Place on egg.

3. Let dry a few minutes, then apply a coat of thinned glue over the picture. Cover the entire surface of the egg, one portion at a time. Let dry to an opaque, porcelain-like finish. Repeat until the coats of glue have covered the picture so well that you cannot feel the edges of the picture.

Variation: The very popular framed three-dimensional découpage can be adapted for Easter eggs displayed on a stand. To create the effect, cut out three exact copies of each picture. Glue the first picture in place, then brush a layer of thinned glue onto the other two pictures and let dry. This makes them stiff. Cut a tiny piece of thin cardboard (such as from a cereal box) for each picture (or several for larger pieces), and glue to the backs of the two pictures to make them thicker and give that 3-D look. Glue the second picture over the first, and the third over the second.

This looks best when only part of each picture is done in this way. For example, if a picture of a basket of fruit is the subject of your découpage, then three-dimensionalize only the fruit and not the basket, or individual fruits and not others.

NATURE EGGS

Even the simplest Nature Eggs have all the charm of a Victorian garden. Carefully arranged pieces are sure to become keepsakes. Depending on your choice of decorations, they can be peeled and eaten if hard-boiled.

1. Arrange on egg until you like the overall effect.

2. Cover a small portion of the egg with glue (or dip in melted wax) and press flowers, etc. into it.

3. When the glue is dry, brush on more coats (as for découpage) until the surface of the egg is smooth.

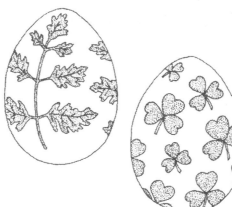

To make, gather:

Clean, dry eggs, raw or hard-boiled, white or pre-dyed

White glue, thinned with water

Artist's paintbrush

Tiny leaves, fresh or dried flower blossoms, grasses, or herbs

YARN EGGS

From the silken sheen of satin to the fuzzy softness of angora, yarn-wrapped eggs vary depending on the character of their coverings. Coil the yarn entirely around the egg or wrap it in patterns, use one color or several, mix textures. It's a fun, easy, inexpensive way to decorate eggs.

Traditional Pennsylvania-Dutch-wrapped eggs were covered with binsegraas, a swamp rush. Fanciful, Polish yarn-wrapped eggs were covered in rug yarn. Today's material choices are many and varied. Consider this partial list and the different effects each type of yarn creates.

- Satin piping
- Knit-Cro-Sheen
- Crewel thread
- Household string rubbed with crayon
- Yarn

- Baby yarn
- Metallic yarn
- Pearl cotton
- Variegated yarn or Knit-Cro-Sheen
- Homespun yarn

Wrapping eggs with yarn is a great way to use yarn scraps from other craft projects. School-age children can master the basic technique in no time and soon can improvise swirls, squiggles, and other interesting patterns.

To make, gather:

Clean, dry, blown eggs

Yarn of your choice, about 4 yards per egg

Glue or rubber cement

Scissors

1. Cover a portion of the egg with glue. If you plan to work a pattern with tight coils, do only a small section at a time. If wrapping the egg from one end to the other, apply glue to a one-inch circle at the top.

2. If working a fancy pattern, lay down straight or border strips of yarn first, then fill in with curves, loops, or other tightly coiled designed. Keep adding glue as needed. Cut yarn longer than you think you will need it for each section, it is much better to snip extra length off when finished gluing a piece than to come up short and have to try and fit in more.

To wrap eggs top to bottom, start by tightly coiling the yarn around one end, and continue wrapping, tightly enough so that the eggshell does not show through, entirely around the egg.

3. Let dry and enjoy.

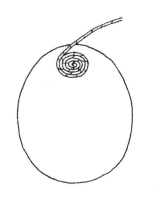

Begin wrapping yarn in a tight circle over the glue-covered end of the egg.

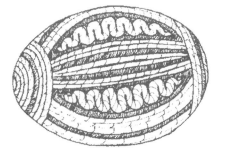

CREPE PAPER EGGS

Bright bits of broken color splash out and surround crepe paper Easter eggs. This is one of the fastest, easiest, and liveliest ways to decorate eggs. The vivid shades of tissue paper bring sparkling life to plain, white eggshell. Whether overlapping in random abandon or carefully placed in a pattern, these fragments of intense colors are real attention getters.

1. Decide on the look you want. It's easy (and quick) to start with a random design and work your way into more complex patterns after that first egg gives you the bug!

2. If working a planned pattern, keep the shapes simple, triangles or squares, and combine in a pleasing order. Basic quilt block patterns are a fine choice, but any type of geometric repetition works well.

   Cut tissue paper shapes by folding paper over itself (up to eight thicknesses) and cutting out all pieces at once. Place the tiny pieces in a dish or bowl, and for heaven's sake, don't sneeze.

   For a random, or Crazy Quilt, cut or tear the pieces into small, irregular shapes.

3. Pour a little glue into shallow dish, and thin with water to the consistency of milk.

4. Brush the thinned glue onto a piece of tissue paper and place it, glue-side down, on the egg. Lightly press into place. Continue gluing, placing, and pressing until the entire egg surface is covered. Overlapping pieces will blend to create new shades. Torn pieces will blend more subtly than the sharp, distinct lines of cut pieces.

   If you are working a pattern with open spots, cover the whole egg first with torn bits of white (or light colored) tissue, let dry a few minutes, then apply the pattern pieces.

5. When dry, apply a coat of spray finish to prevent the dye in the paper from bleeding.

To make, gather:

Clean, dry, blown white eggs

Tissue paper in three or four colors: choose one or two light colors and a dark and a medium shade for high contrast

White glue

Small paintbrush

Shallow container (for thinned glue)

Finish

APPLIQUÉ EGGS

Delicate bits of lace or appliqué dress these eggs in splendid finery. The results are delicately decorated eggs that look as though you spent hours working on them, but which are actually whipped up in minutes.

Appliquéing is a great way for kids to turn out attractive eggs. It is quick, easy, clean, and full of endless possibilities. Even though appliquéd eggs may look too pretty to eat, if food-safe dyes are used, these romantic looking eggs will be a favorite find at any Easter egg hunt.

To make, gather:

Clean, dry eggs, blown or hard-boiled, pre-dyed in bright solid colors

White glue

Bits of lace, rick rack, ribbon or appliqués, including beads and trimmings

Scissors

1. Cut shapes from lace and arrange on a work surface in a nice design.

2. Place a tiny dot of glue on the wrong side of a bit of lace and gently push onto the eggshell. Press for a few seconds, then let dry for a few minutes while preparing the next piece.

3. Glue on any other bits of trim, beads, or sequins.

EGGS OF GOLD & SILVER

Add the glamour of a bowlful of gleaming golden or silver Easter eggs to your spring decor. Talk about a gift for someone who has everything....Actually these eggs aren't exactly priceless works of precious metal, but merely humble eggshells impersonating the eggs of the rich and famous.

The technique is time-consuming but simple, and the results are so real-looking, they always get a second look. Older children love the eye-fooling prank of these solid-metal-looking eggs, especially when someone picks up the nearly weightless hollow shell.

1. Plan a design, and draw it on the eggshell.

2. Cut cardboard into small shapes and glue into place on design to form raised areas. The effect resembles gold (or silver) relief. Glue yarn along lines, curves or in raised swirls, coils, or other designs. Flattened beeswax can be cut into simple shapes with an Exacto knife and adhered to the egg as for wax embossed eggs.

3. Cap the ends of the egg with a 1-inch diameter circle of foil by brushing a small amount of glue, thinned if necessary, to the wrong side of the foil then gently pressing the foil in place. The foil rests loosely over the surface.

4. Take the end of the paintbrush or a flat toothpick, and work the glued foil around the raised areas. Poke, press and smooth the foil until it completely conforms to the contours of the egg. Smooth all areas that lay flat on the egg and all around the edges.

5. Cut a strip of foil wide enough to cover the exposed part of the egg between the capped ends, and long enough to go completely around and meet. For an average chicken egg a piece 2 by 5 inches should suffice. Measure the egg with a bit of string to be sure. Glue the back side of the strip, and lay in place around the egg. Again, work around all the raised areas with the end of the paintbrush or flat toothpick until the foil hugs every bump and ridge. When finished, the egg will look like solid metal with a relief pattern.

6. For a pewter look, brush silver colored foil with a thin coat of black or dark grey paint, and when it is about half dry, wipe with a clean, soft cloth. The residue gives the foil the tone of aged pewter. The same technique can be used with brown paint on gold-toned foil to create a bronzed appearance.

To make, gather:

Clean, dry, blown eggs

Aluminum foil, silver or gold about 4 square inches per egg

Glue

Scraps of string or yarn, thin cardboard or beeswax

Scissors

Paintbrush or flat toothpick

For pewter look, black paint on silver foil

For bronze look, brown paint on gold foil

FAUX FABERGÉ

Tsarina Maria Fydoronva was so grief stricken that she had become gravely ill. It was 1881 and Tsar Alexander II had been murdered. With Easter approaching, the new tsar, Alexander III, turned to the famous jeweler Karl Fabergé to create for his bereaved mother an Easter egg like no other. Fabergé's talents, impeccable standards of workmanship and adventurous originality were the tsar's best hope to cheer the heartsick widow.

A gift of an Easter egg was traditional in nineteenth-century Russia to convey a deep, symbolic meaning of love and faith in the relationship between the giver and the recipient.

On Easter morning the egg, that had been kept a complete secret, was presented to the tsarina who was delighted and amazed. It was so beautiful and intricately designed that she could only gaze in wonder, turning it over and over to admire the elaborate, bejeweled details.

Fabergé was so critical of his own and his apprentices' work that he was said to carry a hammer with him for the sole purpose of smashing any piece of jewelry that did not meet his standards. This devotion to detail put him in good stead with the Russian royal family. Tsar Nicholas II, in keeping with his father's tradition, continued to commission Fabergé to create Easter egg gifts for his own mother and wife. Each year each received a new, fabulously crafted egg of gold and jewels and boundless imagination. It was Fabergé's self-imposed goal to outdo himself each year, often including clever surprises inside the eggs. Over the years he produced more than 50 of these spectacular, cherished eggs, each one striving to be more fantastic than the one before it.

As you may have guessed, cost was of no concern to the imperial Russian tsars. Gold eggs heavily inlaid with rare stones were well within their means. But what your own eggs lack in gold and jewels, you can make up for in imagination. We have already discussed several techniques that can be combined to create equally spectacular-looking eggs. Placed on an ornate egg stand and locked in a glass case, your Faux Fabergé eggs could fool anyone.

Some of the techniques you can incorporate into Faux Fabergé eggs include foil gluing (as in Eggs of Gold and Silver), découpage and simply gluing on phony gems. Another technique, egg cutting, is discussed in Chapter 11 to add a whole new dimension to these already lavish eggs.

1. Decide how detailed your finished egg will be. Sketch a design that strikes you. Découpage, gold braid, pearl trim and glass jewels can transform a plain white egg into a elegant centerpiece. Or use cardboard or beeswax cutouts of different thicknesses beneath gold foil to mimic the image of multi-level gold relief. Arrange small circles of string, or encircling beeswax flower petals beneath the foil to frame glass jewels, making them look inlaid. Fold and glue on bits of foil around each other to form tiny golden roses. Let your imagination fly. Visit your local jeweler or perhaps a museum display for inspiration.

2. For golden Faux Fabergé follow the directions for Eggs of Gold and Silver, but don't stop there. Cut out a tiny portrait or other picture and glue to the egg, perhaps having set up a relief "frame" underneath the foil. Glue a ring of gold braid or strung pearls around the perimeter to camouflage the edges. Glue rhinestones or other bits of fancy to the pattern, working them into your designs as Fabergé did, as the center of a flower, the eye of a snake and so on. Push a corsage pin through the top blow hole as a decorative top piece.

3. You may start with an egg spray painted metallic gold, then add glue on fake jewels, pearls, and trim for beautiful golden eggs without the raised patterns. Or work on a plain white egg, covering with several coats of glue to give the look of porcelain. Decorate eggs pre-dyed in rich jewel shades in the same way for a colorful alternative.

To make, gather:

Clean, dry, blown eggs, white, pre-dyed, or spray painted

Glue

Foil, if desired, and materials to create relief patterns

Découpage picture, if desired

Rhinestones, costume glass jewelry and fake pearls

Tweezers to handle small pieces

Corsage pin

Strung craft pearls, or

Gold-toned braid trim, ribbon, rick rack or other notions

Jewelry-making clasps

BEADWORK EGGS

These gorgeous, intricate eggs were inspired by the timeless beauty of American Indian beadwork. Although there is no evidence they decorated eggs, early Native American cultures rejoiced in the annual return of spring and the new life it brought forth.

To make, gather:

Clean, dry, blown eggs

Beads, strung or individual

Glue

Colored pencils or crayons

Graph paper

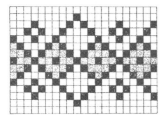

Plot a beadwork design on graph paper.

1. Sketch your design. Graph paper is good for this because it breaks the design into small squares that correspond to each bead in the pattern.

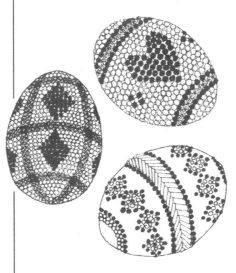

2. Using crayons or colored pencils, draw the design onto the egg. Using the same colors as your beads will give you an easy guide.

3. Either glue the beads to the egg individually or thread the beads on a string, and glue on like yarn (see page 52). Spread glue on the egg, a section at a time and press beads into it. You can work an entire design by feeding beads onto a string (or using pre-strung) beads, wrapping the string around the egg and gluing as for Yarn Eggs. Follow the colors on the design drawn on the egg to recreate the pattern in beadwork.

MORAVIAN STRAW EGGS

The Moravian peasants of long ago worked the fields and farms and had little in the way of worldly goods. But they had a deep desire to honor the Easter observances, and with nothing more than hen's eggs and a few bits of straw created beautiful ornaments. Complex geometric patterns, often following intricate floral themes became a traditional mainstay of their Easter celebrations. The eggs are true keepsakes and collectors' items today, but if you have nimble fingers, imagination, patience, and time, you can create your own old-world treasures.

1. Draw design on paper, then copy onto the egg.

2. Soak a few pieces of straw in warm water for about 20 minutes to soften and make flexible enough to work with.

3. Slit each straw and flatten it out from the inside with a blunt knife blade. Cut small, simple shapes, such as triangles, squares, diamonds, "V"s, strips, or circles from the straw with a sharp scissors.

4. Straw has a shiny side and a dull side, place a dot of glue on the dull side of each cut-out shape, and gently press the straw onto the eggshell in its place in the pattern.

5. Use a straight pin or toothpick to perfectly position each piece. Continue until the design is complete, then let dry.

To make, gather:

Clean, dry, blown eggs, pre-dyed a medium to dark, rich, solid color

Glue or rubber cement

Sharp scissors

Natural straw (available at craft shops)

Shallow bowl of warm water

SPECIAL EFFECTS

CHAPTER 10

n this chapter, you'll be learning how to highlight eggs in several delightful ways. A little paint, a little glue, some construction paper, and some other odds and ends together with your imagination, turn plain-Jane eggs into their personality-plus alter eggos!

PAPER-PUNCH CRITTERS

What do a dinosaur, a quail, a fish, and a duck have in common? If you thought of scales (even birds have scales on their legs, and feathers are actually modified scales) you are onto something. Glue scales to eggs, add a beak, or fins or webbed feet and the character begins to take shape. But cutting out all those scales sounds like a tedious chore, unless you have a paper hole punch.

Kids love to make Swiss cheese out of paper — punching holes until there is nothing left to punch a hole through. While cutting out holes may seem like a goal in itself, in this case it's the dots that the holes make that we want. Instant scales.

Art supply and craft stores are brimming with different kinds of paper that make terrific scales. Construction paper comes in many colors and is easy to handle. The punch goes clean through, leaving crisp, perfect, little circles. The paper is heavy and stiff, though, which can make it difficult to glue down flat against a curved egg. Origami paper, textured papers, glossy or foil lined craft papers, colored copier paper, and a range of others can be used to give your scaly friends that special look. Felt gives a soft, furry look.

Here are a few characters to get you started with paper punch decorating. Experiment with your own ideas for some really eggciting personalities.

Dinosaur Eggs

To make, gather up:

Clean, dry egg — blown or hardboiled
Paper in two contrasting colors
Paper hole punch
Scissors
Glue
Toothpick

1. Copy patterns for head, legs and tails by tracing on a sheet of white paper. Set the white paper over one of the contrasting shades of colored paper. You can copy the pattern onto the colored paper either by tracing over it very hard to create an indented line in the colored paper, or by stapling or taping the two sheets together and cutting along the lines of the traced pattern. Punch out some dots in the contrasting shade for polka-dots.

2. Punch out enough dots in the second color to completely cover the surface of the egg; about one-fourth to one-half of an 8½- by 11-inch piece of paper is enough to cover an egg.

3. Assemble the head and glue it, along with the tail, and legs to the egg as shown. Bend along the dotted lines. Let dry a few minutes before continuing.

4. Put a dot of glue on one paper dot, spread the glue evenly with a toothpick, then using the toothpick to lift it, place the dot over the center of the large end of the egg. (For a blown egg, this should be directly over the blow hole.)

5. Glue more dots around the first one in an overlapping circle, and continue completely around the egg in overlapping, circular rows. Glue dots over the glued-down parts of the head, tail and legs to camouflage them. Work in an occasional dot of another color for polka-dots. Be sure to press down firmly on each dot so that it lies flat against the eggshell and the dots beneath it.

As you approach the small end of the egg, glue a single dot over the center of the end and finish the egg with a circle of dots overlapping the end dot.

6. For triceratops, when the glue is dry, glue legs in place over dots.

St-egg-osaurus

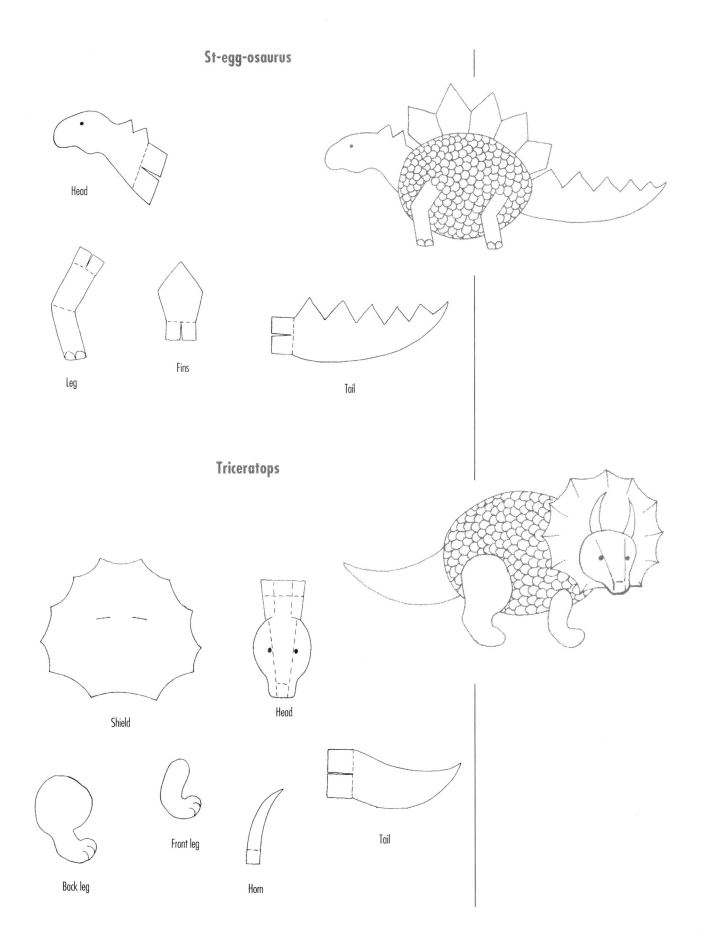

Head

Leg

Fins

Tail

Triceratops

Shield

Head

Back leg

Front leg

Horn

Tail

Quail Egg

To make, gather:

Clean, dry egg, blown or hard-boiled

Paper: brown, grey, black, white, and rust

Paper hole punch

Wiggle-eyes, optional

Scissors

Glue

Four toothpicks

1. Fashion the bill and head plume, and glue in place on egg, bending along dotted lines.

2. Punch out enough dots in grey to cover about one half of the egg, and more in brown, black, and rust.

3. You may want to draw guidelines on the egg first, then following the pattern shown, glue the dots in place over them.

4. Cut out white strips and glue in place.

5. Glue on grey dots or wiggle-eyes for eyes.

6. Cut three toothpicks in half and glue to the bottom of egg as shown for feet.

Plume
(black)

Beak

Face strips
(cut 2)

Just Ducky

To make, gather:

Clean, dry egg, blown or hard-boiled

Paper, yellow and orange

Paper hole punch

Scissors

Toothpick

Beads or wiggle-eyes

Paper umbrella

1. Cut out bill from orange paper according to pattern, bend at dotted lines and glue to egg.

2. Cut duck tail from yellow paper and glue to egg.

3. Punch out enough yellow dots to completely cover egg. Glue on as for dinosaur eggs, hiding the glued portions of the bill and tail.

4. Cut out wing, glue on feather dots as pictured and glue in place. Tuck handle of paper umbrella under one wing as the wing is glued in place.

5. Cut webbed feet from orange paper as in pattern and glue to the bottom of the egg.

6. Glue on beads or wiggle-eyes.

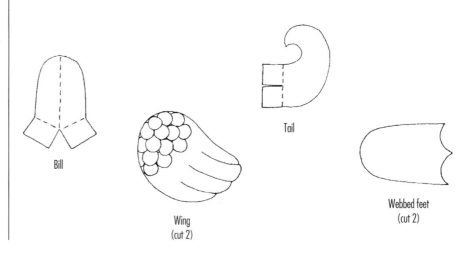

Bill

Wing
(cut 2)

Tail

Webbed feet
(cut 2)

Fishy Egg

1. Cut out fins and tail and glue in place, bending at dotted lines.

2. Punch out enough dots of foil or colored paper to cover the surface of the egg.

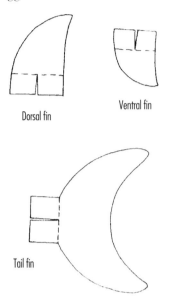

Dorsal fin

Ventral fin

Tail fin

3. Glue the scales in place as for dinosaurs, covering glued down portion of fins.

4. When glue is dry, cut a strip of foil or paper, and glue in place as dividing lines between head and the rest of the body. Draw or glue on eyes and mouth.

To make, gather:

Clean, dry egg, blown or hard-boiled

Aluminum foil: gold for goldfish, or silver for trout, etc.

Or paper, several colors for guppies or rainbow trout, or a single color for a goldfish or other solid colored fish

Or two contrasting shades for a spotted or striped fish

Paper hole punch

Glue

Scissors

Toothpick

Toad Egg

1. Cut out eye pieces as shown, and glue in place, bending at dotted lines.

2. Punch out enough light and dark green dots to completely cover the surface of the egg.

3. Glue wiggle-eyes to the paper eye pieces and glue legs and plastic fly in place.

4. Randomly alternate the light with the dark, and glue in place as for dinosaurs. Draw two nostrils on one

dot and put in place for the nose. Glue a small patch of red paper in place for the mouth, cut out a red tongue, and glue onto the mouth with green scales.

5. Glue purple spots here and there for "warts." Glue on arms.

6. To display, cut a lily pad from some green paper or fabric and place or glue the toad on to it.

To make, gather:

Clean, dry egg, blown or hard-boiled

Paper: light green, dark green, purple, and red

Paper hole punch

Scissors

Toothpick

Wiggle-eyes

Plastic fly

Eye piece
(cut 2)

Arm
(cut 2)

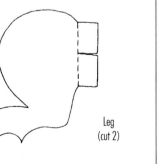

Leg
(cut 2)

To make, gather:

Clean, dry egg, blown or hard-boiled, dyed
    yellow

Paper: yellow and orange

Scissors

Paper hole punch

Four toothpicks

Wiggle-eyes or beads

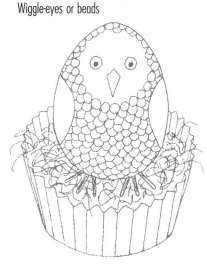

To make, gather:

Clean, dry, blown egg, white or pre-dyed

Paper in a shade corresponding to the main
    color of the bird

Yellow or orange paper for beak

Beads or wiggle-eyes

Paper hole punch

Scissors

Darning needle, small nail or other sharp object
    to poke holes into the hollow eggshell

Tweezers

Jeepers Peepers

1. Cut beak from orange paper and glue in place.

2. Punch out enough yellow dots to cover all of egg but facial area. Glue in place as for dinosaurs, following picture.

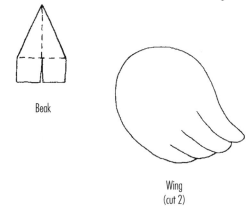

Beak

Wing
(cut 2)

Egg on the Wing

1. Carefully tap three holes into the egg. One on either side for the wings, and one at the rear for the tail. Enlarge holes slightly by lifting out tiny bits of shell with tweezers.

2. Cut wings and tail from paper and fold, accordion-style. Fold one end over itself as shown, and carefully insert into the hole. Repeat for other wing and tail.

3. Cut out wings from yellow paper and glue on.

4. Glue on eyes. Cut three toothpicks in half and glue to bottom of egg as shown for feet.

5. To display, arrange some plastic Easter "straw" in a bird's nest or cupcake liner and place chick inside.

3. Punch out dots to cover all of bird except face and glue in place, as previously described on page 62.

4. Cut out beak and glue in place. Glue on eyes.

5. Bird can be suspended from a piece of monofilament either by gluing it to the back of the bird or by one of the methods described for hanging eggs on page 92.

Wing
(cut 2)

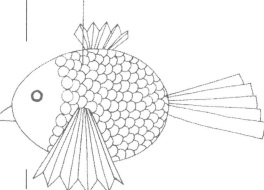

Meggy Mouse

1. Cut out a triangle of cheese from yellow paper; two large round circles from grey paper for outer ear; two smaller circles from white paper for the inner ears; two front legs, two back legs, and a tail from grey paper; and a small triangle for a nose from pink paper. Monofilament, thin wire, or thin strips of grey paper can be fashioned into whiskers.

2. Glue inner and outer ear pieces together and glue to egg, bending at the dotted line.

3. Punch out enough grey dots to cover all of egg except for face and belly areas. Punch out enough white dots to cover tummy and one pink dot for belly button.

4. Glue white pieces in an oval for belly.

5. Snip two slits into each grey dot and glue to body for the coat.

6. Glue tail to underside of body. Glue on legs and cheese. The back legs should balance the egg as a stand.

7. Glue on eyes and draw or glue on whiskers. Glue the small pink nose triangle over the point where the whiskers cross.

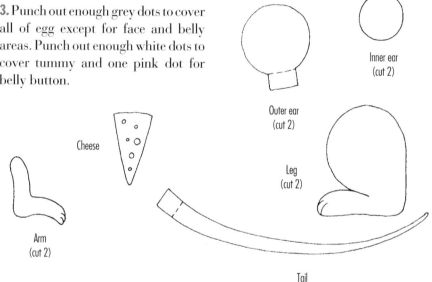

Cheese

Arm
(cut 2)

Outer ear
(cut 2)

Inner ear
(cut 2)

Leg
(cut 2)

Tail

To make, gather:

Clean, dry egg, blown or hard-boiled

Paper: grey, white, yellow, and pink

Scissors

Paper hole punch

Glue

Toothpick

Wiggle-eyes or beads for eyes

Ladybug Egg

1. Pencil in lines to divide head and body and wings.

2. Paint head, dividing lines between wings and spots black.

3. If desired, paint the underside of the bug brown.

4. Paint white markings on head. (Without them, it's a Mexican bean beetle, not a ladybug!)

5. Cut out and glue on legs and antennae.

6. Apply the finish of your choice.

Variation: Instead of paint use hole punch dots from black paper for the dots on the wings.

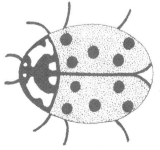

To make, gather:

Orange-dyed egg, blown

Paint, black, white, and brown, if desired

Paintbrush

Black construction paper

Scissors

Glue

Pencil

Hole punch for variation

Finish

COMPOSITE CRITTERS

With nothing more than a few scraps of paper, a dab of glue and some odds and ends, still more endearing characters can be coaxed from an ordinary egg. Here are a few more to try.

Gumdrop Pig or Eggy Sue

To make, gather:

Clean, dry egg, blown or hard-boiled, dyed pink

Six pink gumdrops

Black beads or wiggle-eyes

Small, sharp knife

Glue or icing (the kind sold for decorative writing on frosting)

1. Cut off the wide end of four of the gumdrops so that the sticky gum candy inside is exposed. Make a small slit in the opposite end for the piggy's cloven hooves. Press into place on the "bottom" of the egg. If gumdrop won't stick, use icing or glue to secure.

2. Cut another gumdrop in half and press one end onto the "front" of the egg for the piggy's snout. Push two holes into the gumdrop with a toothpick to resemble nostrils.

3. Remove the bottom of the last gumdrop to expose the sticky candy and slit in half lengthwise. Press one half onto either side of the piggy's head for ears.

4. Carve a coil from the remaining one half gumdrop (left over from making the snout) and press onto the rear of the piggy for a tail.

5. Glue on eyes.

Hatchlings

To make, gather:

Decorated eggshell, broken at one end or along one side. This is a great way to salvage any eggs that are damaged when being blown out after decorating.

Miniature figurine, small enough to fit in eggshell.

Small nest or paper cupcake liner.

1. Carefully lift out broken shell until the opening is large enough for the figurine to emerge from it.

2. Glue egg in place in nest or cupcake liner. If using liner, add some nesting material, such as plastic Easter straw.

3. Place figurine inside egg with one end coming through the opening.

Egghead Clowns

1. Glue fluff in place as hair, leave the top of the head bald.

2. Draw or paint on read cheeks, a mouth, and clown "make-up."

3. Glue on wiggle-eyes and bead nose.

4. Cut a bow tie from fabric or paper and glue near the bottom of the egg. This stabilizes the egg and serves as a stand. Or, cut a pair of shoes from construction paper and glue to the bottom of the egg.

Variations: Egghead people are everywhere. Take ideas from people you see and use them for egg characters. Tiny paper hats, clothes, shoes, and other props bring real personality to egghead people. Create a whole classroom or town full, complete with doll furniture or a construction-paper backdrop for an egg-citing Easter diorama.

To make, gather:

Clean, dry egg, blown or hard-boiled

Felt-tip pens or paints in various colors and brushes

Wiggle-eyes

Large red bead for a nose, or other assorted beads, notions, rick-rack, yarn, or fabric scraps.

Scrap of stiff fabric or construction paper

Glue

Cotton ball or other fluff for hair

Cowboy
Eggbeet

Eggdwina

Clown

Hula Egg

Eggelica

Hayseed Egg

Mom

Rosebud

To make, gather up:

Red dyed egg — blown

Sharp tool for egg scratching, such as a single-edged razor blade

Stiff wire, old coat hanger or craft wire, about 10 inches long

Florists' tape, green

Glue

Green construction paper

Scissors and pinking shears

Wire cutters

Bud vase

1. Using sharp instrument scratch in rose petals.

2. Thread wire through blow holes from bottom of rose bud. Pull through an inch or two and crimp top, as shown, to hold wire in place while you are working.

3. Cut three- or five-petaled leaves from construction paper. Use pinking shears to serrate the edges of the leaves.

4. Cut three to five elongated triangles from florists' tape, as pictured. Holding the wire and egg in one hand, carefully wrap the bottoms of the triangles around the wire. Put a dot of glue on each triangle and press against egg. Hold the glued triangles against the egg for a minute or so while the glue dries.

5. Beginning as close to the triangles as possible, tightly wrap florists' tape around the wire, securing the base of the triangles. Continue about half way down the stem and then wrap in the first leaf. Proceed another inch or two and wrap in the second leaf, facing opposite the first.

6. When glue on triangles is completely dry, use wire cutters to snip off crimp in wire, so that wire does not show above the rosebud.

7. Place the rosebud in a vase and enjoy.

Football

To make, gather:

Clean, dry, blown egg

Brown acrylic paint

White acrylic paint

Sponge

Fine paintbrush

Egg stand

Finish

1. Sponge brown paint onto egg to give a dappled look. Hold the egg between the thumb and forefinger of one hand and apply paint to the middle portion of the egg with the other hand. Let dry on egg stand. When the middle portion of paint is dry, sponge the ends of the egg.

2. When the brown paint is dry, use a fine paintbrush to paint in the lines at either end and the laces.

3. When all paint is dry, apply the finish of your choice.

Note: A fine football egg can also be dyed with the wax-resist method by waxing in the laces on a white egg and dyeing it one coat of brown.

Beehive

1. Draw lines like those circling a beehive around egg as pictured and an opening hole.

2. Tie monofilament or thread to the middle of a one-inch piece of match stick or toothpick and carefully insert one end of the stick into the top blow hole. Push through so that the stick wedges inside of the egg. Tie thread to tree limb.

3. Arrange bees around the hive. Glue one to it and/or suspend others nearby from tree limbs with the thread.

To make, gather up:

Clean, dry, blown egg — use a brown egg or pre-dye or paint a buff or grey color

Black felt tip pen

Branch

Craft bees

Monofilament (clear fishing line) or fine thread

Eggmobile

1. Paint the egg leaving the window areas bare. When paint is dry, you can add passengers "inside" the windows by painting or drawing in place, or by cutting away the shell at the windows and placing small figures inside.

2. Cut plastic wrap to the size of the windows and hold in place with a dot of the finish, such as clear fingernail polish.

3. Cut wheels from paper, and glue in place.

4. Paint macaroni exhaust pipe silver or grey and when dry glue in place.

5. Carefully stick straight pin antenna in place.

6. Apply finish. Vroom!

To make, gather:

Clean, dry, blown egg

Black construction paper

Scissors

Glue

Straight pin with bead end

One piece of small macaroni

Felt-tip pens or paints and brushes

Plastic wrap

Finish

CAMEO EGGS

Think of the small surface of the egg as a miniature artist's canvas. Most of the shell could actually be thought of as the frame, with just a small portion the setting for a scene, portrait or other decoration. Cameo eggs can be very lovely additions to your Easter traditions, especially when a small portrait or silhouette is the subject of the eggshell frame.

To make, gather:

Clean, whole egg, raw or hard-boiled

One shade of dye

Wax (beeswax preferably)

Dyeing cup

White vinegar

Portrait, silhouette cut from fabric or flexible paper using a small photo or appliqué to be framed

Or paints and paintbrush to paint in a scene

Trim, if desired

1. Mix dye according to package or recipe directions.

2. Apply wax to an oval area on one side (both if desired) of the egg. This area will remain white, and be the "canvas" for the portrait, silhouette or scene.

3. Dye egg, and when dye is dry, remove wax as described on page 17, step #4.

4. Cut out portrait or silhouette and glue in place, or simply glue on appliqué. If the scene you are creating is to be hand painted, carefully fill in the picture.

5. When glue or paint is dry, glue trim to edges of dyed area if so desired. Apply finish.

6. If decorating a raw egg, blow the contents out.

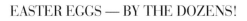

CUT-AWAY EGGS

Decorate a plain, ordinary egg and you create a splendid ornament. But take the decorating process one step further, and you can create intriguing treasures, brimming with delightful surprises. Striving to ever better his last imperial masterpiece, the famous Russian jeweler, Karl Fabergé, incorporated windows, doors and removable tops into some of his most fascinating egg creations. Once exposed, the inside of the egg offers even more possibilities for detailed decoration.

Egg cutting opens up a whole new dimension in egg decorating. You can change the shape, use the inside as a three-dimensional setting for miniature scenes, decorate the inner surface of the shell, make working doors and windows that reveal miniature delights, or create functional items as well as spectacular ornaments. All this, and it's easy to do!

EGG CUTTING

Cutting eggshell is easy. Getting it to look like what you envisioned is a little more demanding. It isn't complicated, it just requires care and patience. Dyes, paints, découpage and more can be used to decorate cut-out eggs. Eggs must be dyed before cutting. Rather than blow cut eggs, simply empty out the contents through the cut-out opening.

Outline the area to be cut out with a pencil or felt-tip pen, poke a small hole with a darning needle or other sharp instrument, and insert the tip of a pair of manicure scissors (the type with the short, curved blades). Cut in short snips, with the curve of the blade facing into the opening being cut. Turn the egg as you cut and follow along the outside of the line so that it is cut away. When an opening has been created, tip the egg over and shake the contents out.

The eggshell will chip somewhat, and the line will most likely not be as perfectly even as hoped for, but the rim can be covered with decoration, so don't worry if it isn't perfect. If the shell shatters or splits excessively, try cutting in shorter snips or cutting more slowly. The fresher the egg the better, since the eggshells of older eggs become brittle.

Removing any part of the shell reduces the eggs ability to withstand handling. To help strengthen the shell, apply a coat of clear or colored fingernail polish, first to the outside shell, and to the inner shell following decoration. Be sure to let fingernail polish dry thoroughly (about 20 minutes) before further handling.

For sophisticated egg designs that include open doors or windows, it is often best to cut two eggs. The egg that forms the body of the design must have a smooth, even opening. Attached doors or windows cut from a second egg can be cut out slightly oversized and trimmed to perfection.

Think of the inside of the eggshell as an extension of the artist's canvas. It may be painted, découpaged, or embellished with glued-on decorations. Before applying any additional decoration, however, peel away the membrane residue and check to be certain the inner surface is dry. Paint or découpage the inside. Glitter makes a wonderful inner shell decoration. To apply, thin white glue with water, then paint onto inner shell with a small paintbrush. Sprinkle in glitter and shake around so that the entire inner surface is coated. Shake out the excess onto a piece of paper. Fold the paper, and guide the extra glitter back into the bottle along the crease. Sequins also make a dazzling inner treatment. Glue the inside of the shell as for glitter, then using tweezers insert the sequins one at a time.

If you wish to make the egg into a hanging ornament, there are two basic ways of attaching a hanger. Anchor it inside the egg through the blow hole, or glue it onto the outside shell. Thin wire or Christmas tree ornament hooks work well for the first type. See section on egg hanging on page 92.

Insert tiny flowers, characters, or scenes by pressing a small amount of clay (florists' clay, salt dough, or kid's dough all work) into the bottom of the egg. The clay raises the scene above the rim of the opening so that it is clearly seen and holds the pieces securely.

For doors or attached windows, cut the pieces from a second eggshell dyed to match. Decorate the pieces on both sides to match the egg's body. Attach the doors by using a small piece of paper, fabric, ribbon, or other decoration as a hinge. Glue a hinge to each door, then glue the other side of the hinge and hold against the body of the egg until the glue has set. The length of the fabric used as the hinge will determine the flexibility of the hinge.

Eggs that are not to be hung may be set on a stand or have a simple stand glued directly to the egg. For more on stands and displaying eggs, see page 92–93.

EASTER EGGS — BY THE DOZENS!

EASTER BASKET EGG

The term "Easter egg basket" takes on a new twist when the basket is cut from a decorated egg. Making this cute miniature basket is easy, yet the finished basket makes a wonderful addition to your holiday settings.

1. Poke blow holes into egg with the top (narrow end) hole being about ¼ inch off center.

2. Draw pencil lines where basket handle is to be cut. Poke a small hole along one side of the handle basket and cut out the opening. Shake out contents of egg, then cut out opposite side. Let inside dry before decorating.

3. The egg may either be pre-dyed and decorated or decorated after the basket shape is cut out. Create a wicker woven effect with felt-tip pens or paints by wrapping with yarn, or by decorating any way you wish.

4. Fill the basket with jelly bean eggs, a single candy kiss, or marshmallow chick, or push a small amount of clay into the bottom to anchor a tiny flower arrangement or miniature figurines.

5. Glue a circle of string or yarn at the base of the basket so that it will set upright.

To make, gather:

Whole raw egg, plain or pre-dyed

Manicure scissors

Felt-tip pens, paints, flowers, ribbons, or other decorations

EGG PLANTER OR VASE

Ah, spring. The resurgence of growth of plants and flowers is synonymous with the season. Introduce plants or flowers to your eggs for a natural link between the season and the symbol.

1. Starting at the narrow end of the egg, cut an opening in the top portion of the shell.

2. Decorate the planter/vase to your taste.

3. If using a flower arrangement, press a small amount of florists' clay into the bottom of the eggshell to hold the flowers in place. Poke the stem of each flower into the clay and wait for the clay to dry.

4. If planting a tiny plant, bulb, or seeds, poke a hole in the bottom of the egg and enlarge to ⅛ inch by carefully picking out tiny bits of shell. Thoroughly wet fine potting soil and gently press into eggshell. The eggshell should be about ⅔ full. Set seeds, bulb, or plant into shell. Be careful to cover any roots. Let egg planter rest on napkin ring or other stand, in a sunny window.

To make, gather:

Blown egg, plain or pre-dyed

Manicure scissors

Napkin ring or other stand

Choice of tiny dried or silk flowers, a small plant such as an air fern, a small bulb such as a crocus, or seeds

Florists' clay or potting soil

Decorations of choice

 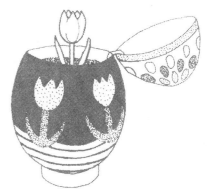

TULIPS

One of the first signs of spring is the joyful unfurling of spring flowering bulbs, including tulips. Whether subtle in color or bright and brash, the stately tulip has long been a springtime favorite. In fact, tulips were at one time more valuable a commodity than gold in certain European markets and the secrets of breeding them kept as closely guarded as any secrets of state. Enjoy their splendor at this special season, or all year long by developing a delicate, colorful strain of your own.

To make, gather:

Pre-dyed eggs in deep, vivid colors

Florists' wire or other stiff wire (a straightened clothes hanger will do)

Florists' tape

Glue

Manicure scissors

Scissors

Felt-tip markers or paints

Vase or planter

Florists' clay or plaster of Paris for securing stems in planter

Moss

Green construction paper for leaves

Sharp tool, such as single-edged razor for scratching dye (optional)

Pencil

Finish

1. Draw lines to be cut to open the top of the tulip blossom. Scratch lines to show separate petals, if desired.

2. Poke a small hole into narrow end of egg, insert manicure scissors blade, and carefully cut away area between pencil lines. Shake out contents of egg. Let inside dry completely before continuing.

3. Use felt-tip pens or paints to paint in accents such as splashes of color or a different color rimming the edges of the petals. Paint interior of shell, if desired, complete with pistils and stamen. If petals were not divided by scratching, use a deeper shade than the dye of the egg to paint or draw in petal dividing lines. Apply finish.

4. Cut three or four triangles from florists' tape. Insert the end of the wire into the bottom blow hole, and crimp it over itself to prevent it from sliding back through the hole. Wrap the bottom ends of the triangles around the wire, as close to the tulip blossom as possible, and apply a dot of glue to each. Press the glued triangles (sepals) onto the tulip and hold, for at least a minute, while the glue dries.

5. Wrap the remainder of the stem with florists' tape. If you will be placing the tulips in a vase, wrap tape all the way to the end of the wire. If arranging tulips in a planter, leave the bottom few inches (the length to be under the "soil level" in the planter) exposed.

6. Apply finish to the egg.

7. If displaying your tulips in a vase, arrange them to suit your eye. A block of florists' foam, cut to shape and inserted in the vase, will stabilize the bouquet and hold it in place indefinitely.

8. If using a planter for a springtime display, fill ⅔ of the way with florists' clay or plaster of Paris and arrange stems. Camouflage clay or plaster with moss.

9. Arrange leaves, cut from construction paper or taken from silk flowers, in with the stems, for a natural look.

Variation: An easy alternative to fashioning stems and leaves is to purchase silk (or plastic) tulips and pull the flower heads off. The stems can then be used, leaves and all, for homemade tulips.

MINIATURE FURNISHINGS

Anyone who owns a dollhouse or collects miniatures will love to include any of the following three pieces in their collection. Other possibilities abound, limited only by what you can envision.

Teeny, Tiny Tiffany

1. Sketch stained-glass pattern onto eggshell, and fill in the design with pens, paints, or glued on bits of crepe paper.

2. Apply finish over ink or paint, one section at a time, and let dry.

3. Pipe on a line of black fabric writer, stained-glass leading, or blackened beeswax in between each patch of color for the leaded stained-glass effect.

4. Poke a hole into the end of the egg opposite the stained glass design, insert the tip of manicure scissors, and carefully snip away the shell from the lamp shade design. Empty the contents. When finished cutting, don't worry if you need to touch up the edges with "leading."

5. If desired, cut fringe from pearl cotton or other string and glue to the bottom rim of lamp shade.

6. If making a hanging shade, carefully poke a small hole through the center of the lamp and feed in a small length of fine chain. Glue in place. Chain may also be secured by pushing the end through a small piece of construction paper and gluing the paper to the eggshell.

To make, gather:

Whole egg

Felt-tip pens, paints, or crepe paper

Paintbrush

Black fabric writer, stained glass leading, or blackened beeswax and kistka

Manicure scissors

Fine chain for a hanging lamp or a lamp stand for a free-standing lamp. (Candlesticks or doll furniture make acceptable stands.)

Pearl cotton or other decorative string

Glue

Finish

Cradle

1. Hold egg lengthwise, and pencil in lines. Insert point of scissors through blow hole and cut away open area. Empty contents.

2. Glue feet to cradle, making certain the cradle rests squarely on them.

3. Decorate cradle with lace, ribbon, or other decorations.

4. Glue a flounce of fabric around the base of the cradle.

5. Fold and glue baby blankets inside of cradle and place a tiny toy baby inside.

To make, gather:

Whole egg, plain or pre-dyed

Manicure scissors

Lace, ribbons, and other decorations

Four large beads or pieces of molded clay for legs

Six to eight inches of "baby fabric"

Glue

Bathtub

To make, gather:

Whole egg, white or pre-dyed

Manicure scissors

Feet molded from clay or salt dough (See page 83 for salt dough recipe.)

1. Holding egg lengthwise, draw a line around the egg dividing the top and bottom halves. Poke a small hole at some point along the line, insert tip of scissors and carefully cut egg in half. Empty contents.

2. Affix legs. If clay is still wet, press onto egg and let dry. If legs are already dry, glue in place.

You may also use a small amount of clay or salt dough to fashion tiny faucets and handles and paint them to match.

EGG JEWELRY & OTHER ODDITIES

What better baubles than big, beautiful (egg) beads? Inexpensive jewelry making supplies can turn shy shells into dangling decorations for big kids and tiny tykes alike. Of course, the hollow shells are fragile and may not survive their fashion debut, but a careful wearer can sport a real conversation starter.

Hobby and craft stores stock many items for jewelry making that will quickly convert decorated eggshells into unusual earrings, a pendant, a necklace, or a whopper of a ring. First decorate the egg to suit your fancy, apply a shiny finish (both for luster and added shell strength), and add the appropriate jewelry setting.

JEWELRY

Earrings: Craft stores sell earring settings for jewelry making, bell caps, and other pieces that can be glued to the egg. Glue or wire earring settings directly to the egg, bell cap, or other fixture that has been glued to the egg. An alternative is to use old (or cheap) earrings. Glue or wire eggs in place, depending on the style of the existing earrings. An easy and attractive way to prepare eggs for earring (or pendant) mountings is to feed a wire or thread through the blow holes and attach a large, decorative bead (that won't slip back through the hole) at each end.

Pendants: Pendant mountings can be purchased in craft stores, but it is easy and inexpensive to thread a piece of narrow ribbon (string or yarn) through the holes and knot (or tie to a large bead) at the bottom of the egg.

Necklace: Make an egg and bead necklace by threading string, yarn, or monofilament alternately through decorated eggs and large beads. Tie each end of the string to a necklace clasp or make the necklace long enough to fit over the wearer's head.

Ring: Make heads turn with the biggest ring gem in town! For a simple setting, glue a piece of paper to a dimestore ring and glue the egg to the paper. Try gluing an egg directly to a ring setting with a "super" glue.

If you would like to create some egg jewelry on a less grand scale or of a less fragile nature, follow the instructions on page 83 for homemade salt dough. Roll the dough into egg shapes of whatever size you choose, insert a toothpick or straw for a hole, dry, or bake and decorate.

Other egg oddities you may like to try include confetti eggs and mariachi eggs. Both are fun for kids, big and small.

CONFETTI EGGS

To make, gather:

Blown eggs, white or pre-dyed

Confetti (available at party supply houses)

Decorations

Colored paper and glue

1. Make sure egg is totally dry. Enlarge one blow hole by carefully picking out tiny bits of shell.

2. Fold a piece of paper into a small funnel and feed confetti into enlarged hole.

3. Cut out a small piece of the colored paper and glue over enlarged hole.

Fashion the paper to look like part of the overall egg design.

4. As a magic trick hold up the egg in one hand. Quickly close your fist around the egg and toss the contents into the air. The egg "disappears" (is crushed) and bits of confetti (and unnoticed eggshell) fly everywhere.

MARIACHI EGGS

1. Proceed as for Confetti Eggs, but fill with unpopped popcorn, dried beans or rice.

2. Glue the large end to a colored, wooden golf tee (the curve of the tee cradles the curve of the egg perfectly). Let dry and cha cha cha!

EGGSHELL MOSAICS

To make, gather:

Broken eggshells

Dye and cups

Egg carton to hold eggshells

Tweezers

Piece of cardboard or other object to be decorated

Glue

Have fun, create a unique craft project and salvage any eggshell accidents by using broken bits of shell for unusual eggshell mosaics.

1. Dye broken eggshells in various colors. Spread the pieces out on a paper towel to dry.

2. Break the eggshell pieces into small bits, about ⅛ inch across. Use the separate compartments of an egg carton or other divided container to hold the various colored mosaic pieces, just as an artist uses a palette.

3. Draw a design onto the piece of cardboard or object to be decorated.

Outline the design, if you like, by gluing yarn along the outside lines.

4. Apply glue to an area that is to be covered with one color of eggshell, then, using tweezers to grip the tiny pieces of eggshell, fill the area in with bright bits of mosaic color.

5. When the design is dry, spray on a coat of finish to protect it and add shine.

FAKE EGGS

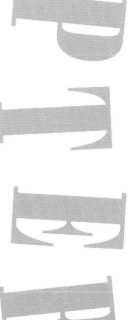

ot all wonderful eggs start with a chicken. Duck eggs, turkey, goose, and even ostrich eggs make fabulous raw materials for egg projects. But there are other eggs to consider, each lending its own, very unique and special properties to your decor. In fact, some very beautiful eggs require little or no participation from the real thing.

QUILTED EGGS

Snoop around any local craft or sewing shop and you will soon discover that plastic foam comes in egg shapes, in a range of sizes. Add a few scraps of fabric, bits of ribbon or lace, and a few minutes of your time, and you have the makings of charming country-quilted eggs. The surprisingly simple technique doesn't require a needle and thread. It doesn't require a glue gun or any other special tools. Making beautiful plastic foam eggs is easy enough for children and fun and rewarding enough for all ages.

To make, gather:

Plastic foam egg (any size)

Fabric scraps in solid colors or a small print (a 5 x 10 scrap covers a 2¼ inch egg)

Scissors

Metal fingernail file

Bits of ribbon, lace or rick rack

Crochet hook (if making a hanging egg)

Monofilament or narrow ribbon for hanging

Glue

1. Draw a quilt pattern onto the egg's surface. Try an easy pattern, such as sectioning the egg into vertical quarters or sixths, or dividing it horizontally. The larger the egg, the more varied the quilt design possibilities.

2. For each section cut a piece of fabric to size, plus about ½ inch bigger all the way around. Alternate different colors or prints in the pattern.

3. If you are making a hanging egg ornament, the first step is to attach the hanger. A pretty and simple hanger can be made with narrow ribbon and a crochet hook. Push the hook through the egg, starting at the narrow end and coming out of the wider end. Catch a piece of ribbon in the hook and pull it back through in a loop. Tie the ends in an overhand knot and pull the loop until the knot rests snugly against the bottom of the egg.

   An alternative hanger is made the same way with monofilament. Knot the line around a decorative bead, large enough not to slip back through the hole made by the crochet hook.

4. Using the pointed tip of the fingernail file, score along the lines of the quilt pattern. Indent the plastic foam about ⅛ of an inch completely around each section.

5. Place a cut piece of fabric over the section it is to cover. Position it so that it fits exactly over the section with about ¼ inch extra fabric extending past the lines all the way around. Use the point of the fingernail file to push the ¼ inch overage into the scored lines in the plastic foam. Turn the egg as you work, pushing the fabric into the egg all the way around the patch. You can push the fabric quite deeply into the egg, so don't worry if the overage is somewhat more than ¼ inch. Do be careful, however, that you don't create wider holes than necessary; the fabric may slide out, and the holes are difficult to hide.

6. Cover each section with fabric, using a different color or print for each section or alternating colors with prints. Once the entire egg is covered with "quilting," you may add ribbon, lace, rick rack, or other decorations with a small amount of white glue.

Dough Art

Charming salt-dough creations have graced country kitchens the world over. Homemade dough art offers a warm, rustic appeal that changes ordinary household items, such as jar lids and refrigerator magnets, into fanciful folk art. The different textures you can produce, along with the rainbow of colors available in food colorings or paints, makes this an especially versatile medium. Finished dough-art creations can last indefinitely if handled with care. With so much going for this fun and fanciful craft, what egg decorator could do without it?

Salt-Dough Recipe

1. Mix dry ingredients first, then add water, oil and mix well into as stiff dough.

2. Pat into a ball and knead by hand until the dough is smooth and satiny.

3. To color, tear off bits of dough and work in food coloring (paste or liquid) until the dough is evenly colored. Or, leave the dough its natural color, and when your project has been sculpted and dried, paint by hand with acrylics.

4. Refrigerate unused dough in a covered container.

Dough-art projects can be air dried or baked at about 250°F. for an hour or two on a foil-covered cookie sheet. Let the piece dry (and cool) completely, into a hard, brittle pottery before painting or finishing. Colored doughs are more subtle than those that are painted because the color is part of the sculpture. Paints, however, provide clear, bright colors that can't be matched with food-colored dough. Finish with a coat of lacquer to protect it from moisture and to give a warm shine.

To make, gather:
2 cups flour
1 cup salt
½ cup water
¼ cup salad oil

To make, gather:

Clean, dry, blown egg

Recipe of salt dough

Food coloring or paints and brushes

Some of the following:

> Paper clips for hangers
>
> Toothpicks, straws, etc. to indent dough
>
> Beads, sequins, feathers, brush bristles or short strands of monofilament for whiskers on characters

Tweezers to handle small pieces

Rolling pin or round glass or jar for working the dough

Pinking shears or garlic press for special effects

Small knife for trimming ends

Plastic bag and container to store dough in

Spray finish

Dough-Dough Egg

1. Prepare the dough and color portions of pink, yellow, blue or your favorite Easter shades. Leave ¼ to ½ of the dough in its natural color for the eggshell. If you wish to make a colored (similar to a dyed) egg, color a large portion of the dough in the shade of your choice.

If you choose to hand paint the finished egg, omit the coloring step. A word of caution: even though bright, hand-painted projects are eye catching, they're time consuming. Once a piece is formed and put in place, dry and apply a coat or two of finish.

2. When the dough is smooth, roll out a thin sheet in the body color. Cut a piece large enough to envelope the entire egg — approximately 2 by 5 inches for an average egg.

3. Fit the dough around the egg, smoothing it down evenly as you go. With a small, sharp knife trim excess dough from the egg ends. Where ends of the piece of dough meet, dab a little water onto the edges and press together to "glue" them in place.

4. Form flower petals, leaves, vines, letters for names, chicks, bunnies, a cross, or any Easter scene from the colored dough. Use pinking shears to create zigzags, or force the dough through the garlic press to make long strands for vines, hair, etc. Form each feature, one at a time, dab a drop of water onto the back side, and gently press it into place. For a free-standing egg, roll out a long, thin coil of dough with your palm, dampen the bottom of the dough wrapped egg, and circle the coil of dough around the bottom end. Before drying (or baking) the egg, press down gently so that the dough ring at the bottom conforms to a flat surface.

5. With all the decorations in place, dry in well-ventilated spot or place on a foil-covered cookie sheet in a 250°F. oven for about an hour. When completely dry and cooled, apply one or two coats of spray finish.

Refrigerator Magnets

Whimsical refrigerator magnets have a homespun appeal and an undeniable practicality. Extend the special season of spring all year round, make adorable gifts or just use up that extra salt dough with cute, colorful magnets that are as easy to make as they are to love.

1. Roll out dough about ¼-inch thick. Cut out egg shapes or other Easter symbols with a sharp knife or cookie cutters. You can add a three-dimensional effect by pressing down the edges while allowing the middle to round up.

2. Place each cut-out shape over a magnet on the foil-lined cookie sheet. Press down lightly to imbed the magnet in the dough. The dough is fairly heavy, so be sure to use a big enough magnet (or several small magnets) to be strong enough to hold it up (plus the notes and what-have-you that refrigerator magnets are used for).

3. Embellish your characters as you please with formed pieces of dough or other accessories. Remember to wet the back of each feature before pressing it in place.

4. Bake or let dry until hard as a rock. Paint if using uncolored dough. Apply finish.

To make, gather:

Salt dough, colored with

Food coloring or paints and brushes

Spray finish

Small magnets available at craft shops

Foil-lined cookie sheet for drying

Any of the suggestions listed under Dough-Dough Eggs

Decorated egg magnets made from dough

PAPIER MÂCHÉ EGGS

Papier mâché is an age-old craft. It has stayed popular in great part because the materials needed — paper and paste — are cheap and always available. No special instruments and no toxic chemicals are required. But the best part is that it's good, clean — well, actually sort of slimy — fun.

To make, gather:

An egg-shaped frame on which to build the paper egg, from a giant egg on a frame of flexible poultry wire (available at feed and farm stores) to a good-sized "ostrich" egg on a balloon frame.

Old newspapers, torn into ¾-inch strips

Wallpaper paste

Large container for mixing the paste

Stick or spoon for stirring

Paints and brushes

Flowers, etc. to glue on

1. Tear, do not cut, the newspaper into strips. Torn pieces blend better at the edges. If the paper is difficult to tear, turn the sheet and tear crosswise. Trying to tear against grain of newsprint will result in uneven strips and frustration.

2. Mix the paste per package instructions.

3. Blow up an oval balloon. Do not overfill the balloon with air as papier mâché has a tendency to shrink as it dries and the pressure may burst a taut balloon before the paper is dry enough to hold its shape.

4. Place several strips of paper into the paste and swirl around with your hand (might as well get used to how this stuff feels) until all are well coated with the slippery solution. Pull the strips out, one at a time and slide between two fingers to remove excess paste.

5. Lay the wet paper strips across the balloon, in one direction, until the surface is totally covered. Then, alternate a layer of strips going in the opposite direction. Smooth the papers down with your hands, until the surface of the egg is as even as possible. Let dry overnight.

6. To decorate, first paint the entire surface of the egg in a white or pastel base coat. Two or more coats of paint may be necessary to cover the newsprint. Then paint, print, or stencil any designs you can dream of onto your king-sized egg.

Variation: Carefully cut the dried egg in half before decorating it. Cut a strip of lightweight cardboard, about ½-inch wide and long enough to go completely around the egg where it was cut. Glue the strip in place inside one half of the egg. This will act as a lip to hold the halves together. You may wish to camouflage the lip by applying a layer of papier mâché inside of that half of the egg, blending it in with the edge of the lip.

Decorate both the inside and outside of your giant egg, or use the hidden compartment to surprise someone with a gift.

DISPLAYING & STORING EGGWORKS

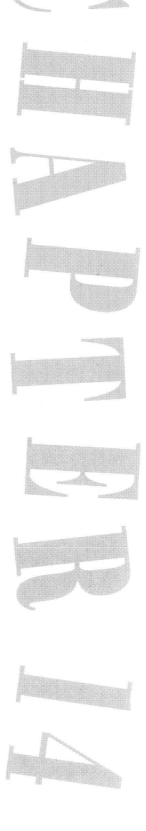

O nce your creative touch has forever transformed a humble egg into an objet d'art, you will want to display it to its best advantage, and to cherish it for years to come. Eggs can be beautifully displayed in many different ways, and if carefully handled and stored, will last for generations.

EGGS ON DISPLAY

Just as different customs for decorating eggs have evolved throughout the world, so have display methods. One such lovely custom originated when Swiss and German country folk heralded spring by attaching decorated eggs to the tree branches and bushes near their homes. The practice soon moved indoors, with a small tree or branch being set up in a special place and covered with decorated eggs. By the 1890s Easter egg trees, laden with ornate and elaborate decorations, had become a popular German tradition. Gloriously decorated eggs (often filled with candy treats), glass figurines, tinsel and cookies or cakes in the shape of bunnies and lambs, overflowed the boughs of the egg tree. Like another German tree decorating tradition, this custom soon migrated around the globe.

Egg Tree

Though the original German versions were most often evergreen, bare limbs serve best for eggs-hibiting Easter art. A large tree can be set up just like a Christmas tree, while a small tree or a branch makes perfect counter top or centerpiece displays.

To make, gather:

Tree or branch with several evenly spaced branches

Pruning shears

Old coffee can or planter for tree base, or Christmas tree stand

Plaster of Paris or florists' clay to weigh down the tree base and secure the tree or branch in place.

Foil or spray paint to decorate base

Blown, decorated eggs

Ornaments, including salt dough "cookies" in the shape of bunnies, chicks, or other Easter symbols.

1. You can spray paint the tree or branch with a coat of white or pastel paint. Take the tree outside or into a well-ventilated area, protect the floor and surrounding area with newspapers and spray away. Let dry completely before securing into stand or base. If you prefer the natural look, omit this step.

2. If using a salvaged can, etc. for a base, decorate it with foil (see Eggs of Gold and Silver for some special tips) or spray paint. Let dry.

3. Mix plaster of Paris according to package directions and fill the container about half full. Position the end of the branch into the wet plaster, and fill the container while holding the branch in place. Hold or prop the branch in place until the plaster has set. Alternatively press a piece of florists' clay large enough to nearly fill the container, and firmly push the branch into place. As the clay dries, the branch will be locked into place. A layer of moss or plastic "grass" will hide either material attractively.

Enjoy a fresh branch or tree, complete with spring buds and maybe even a few new leaves by using a water reservoir Christmas tree stand.

4. Once the tree or branch is firmly held in place, tie your eggs and decorations into the branches and admire it all.

Homemade Tree

Egg trees of various sizes, shapes and designs can be purchased through gift catalogues and shops. Usually they come apart for storage and resemble familiar spring characters as much or more than actual trees. Follow this simple pattern and general directions to make an egg tree that you can use and appreciate for years to come.

1. Enlarge pattern to the size of tree you wish to make.

2. Cut out pattern, place over plywood and trace design.

3. Cut pattern. Sand until smooth.

4. Paint tree as desired. Assemble when paint is dry.

5. Hang eggs from branches and enjoy!

To make, gather:

¼-inch plywood, amount depends on size of tree you wish to build

Skillsaw, jigsaw, or neighbor with either

Sandpaper

Paints and brushes

EGG MOBILES

Another intriguing way to display a batch of your finest eggs is to build an egg mobile. Decorated eggs float on air as they counterbalance each other, swaying and bobbing with the gentlest breeze.

Although various designs can be devised incorporating materials at hand, the basic parts of a mobile are simple: arms, or crossarms, to hang the decorations from; decorations to hang; and line to tie it all together.

Make arms from lightweight materials. The only prerequisite is that the arms be evenly sized, so that one end is no heavier than the other. Examples include thin dowels found in art supply, hardware and pet stores; stiff, heavy wire, such as old hangers and lightweight pipe or stiff tubing.

Your mobile design will determine the length and number of arms. A few basic configurations make good starting points for experimentation. The most important thing is balance. Cut the arms in successive lengths, beginning with the shortest arms first. For instance, for the designs pictured, start with a 4-inch arm, then a 6-inch arm, then 8- and finally a 10-inch arm. By following the shorter arms with longer arms you can prevent balancing problems.

To make, gather:

Arm or crossarm material, cut to size

Hanging line, monofilament, ribbon, or fancy thread all work beautifully

Decorated eggs

1. Use the hanging line to tie the eggs to the ends of the arms. Each arm should have an egg at each end, except for the bottom-most arm which may also suspend an egg from the center. Make certain that the arm is balanced by looping a length of hanging line around the arm and lifting up. If the arm hangs level from the line, then the eggs are balanced. If it tips down in one direction, then there is more weight at that end. Since you can't change the weight of the eggs, adjust the line until you find the exact balance point, then permanently tie the line there. String eggs singly from the line or suspend in twos or threes (see Egg Hanging Techniques, page 92).

2. Once all the arms balance individually, tie the bottom arm to the next one up, using the same technique to balance it that you used for balancing eggs individually. When you can hold the two arms suspended from a line, in perfect balance, tie them to the arm above them. When all arms are attached to each other, find the center of balance on the top most arm, tie the line to it, and tie a loop at the end of the line.

3. Go hang it up!

EASY EGG MOBILE

If balancing and tying several arms of a mobile together sound like more bother than you may be willing to put up with, there is an easier way. By recycling a large coffee can or other circular or cylindrical object, you can quickly construct a swirl of delight with decorated eggs.

1. Using hammer and nail or hole punch, depending on the material of the hanging base, punch holes at regular 2-inch intervals around the bottom rim of the coffee can (body of the mobile), and in the center of the top.

2. Decorate the can in a design to match those of the eggs.

3. When the decorations are dry, tie the eggs into the holes. Tie the first egg about 4 inches from the bottom of the body of the mobile and each successive egg about 2 inches lower than the one before it.

4. Thread a hanging line through the hole in the top of the can, and tie it around a broken stick or other object too large to fit back through the hole.

5. Hang it up and admire.

Use old clothes hangers cut to length, and bend ends into loops for tying eggs.

Balance — both visually and in weight — is the key.

To make, gather:

Decorated eggs, ready for hanging, using any of the methods described on page 92

Discarded coffee can or other cylinder

Paints and brushes or foil to decorate above

Nail or hole punch

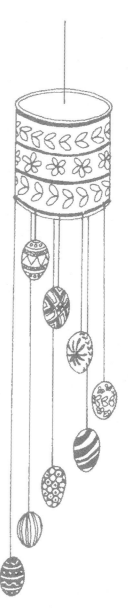

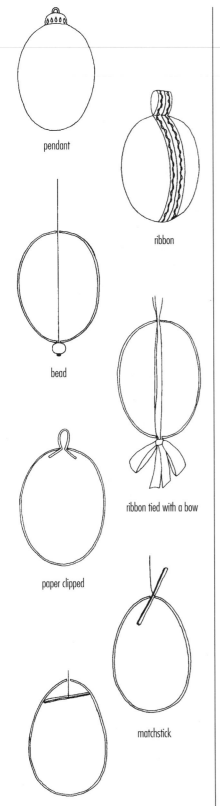

pendant

ribbon

bead

ribbon tied with a bow

paper clipped

matchstick

EGG HANGING TECHNIQUES

There are several ways to attach a line to a blown egg, be it invisible monofilament, ribbon, thread, or yarn. Here are but a few suggestions for the hanging party:

Pendant mounting: Glue pendant mount, bell caps, or fancy-looking jewelry accessories onto egg. Craft shops carry these jewelry making specialty items, and old dimestore or costume jewelry pieces can be recycled.

Ribbon: Glue a loop of ribbon or lace to the sides of an egg and extend over the top. Glue a short loop of ribbon to the top of the egg. (This also works with plastic foam eggs.)

Bead: Glue an open bead to the top of an egg and run a thin line through it. Run a line through the hollow egg and tie to a large bead at the bottom.

Matchstick: Break wooden match sticks or toothpicks into pieces small enough to fit through the blow hole, and wedge inside the narrow end.

Tied with a bow: Using a very small crochet hook or darning needle, pass a length of ribbon, yarn, or lace through the egg and pull out the bottom end. Be sure to use a long enough piece to tie in an attractive bow.

Paper clipped: Snip a paper clip in half so that it resembles an elongated "U". Bend the ends of the "U" in opposite directions and feed through a slightly enlarged blow hole in opposite directions.

Almost any lightweight, attractive line can be used to hang Easter eggs. Here are a few to try:

Monofilament: Invisible.

Yarn: Colorful, inexpensive.

Ribbon: Colorful, elegant, available in varying widths.

Lace: Romantic, sophisticated, in varying widths.

Knit-Cro-Sheen: Colorful, inexpensive — try crocheting a chain of solid colored or variegated cord or macramé a twisting cord by tying a length of half-knots.

Satin piping: Regal, in elegant colors.

String: Cheap, can be colored with crayon.

Pipe cleaner: Make a fragile, but functional hook with a half length of pipe cleaner, by bending a hook in one end, passing it through the blow hole and gently pulling up to catch the hook. Twist a loop in the top portion.

Strung beads or pearls: Elegant, available in a range of lustrous colors.

WREATHS

A lovely way to display a collection of decorated eggs is to work them into a springtime wreath. Wrap a wooden or plastic foam wreath with strips of fabric or raffia, and glue eggs in place or bend a wire hanger into a circle and bind overlapping bunches of dried flowers or herbs to it until the circle is covered. Pass a piece of monofilament through the two blow holes of several eggs, nestle each egg tightly into the foliage, pass the line to the backside of the wreath, and tie the eggs in place. Tie or glue eggs to any existing wreath.

BASKETS

One classic way of displaying Easter eggs is to snuggle them into Easter baskets. Place eggs among sprigs of dried or silk flowers, or arrange your collection on a bed of straw or plastic Easter "grass." Tuck Easter eggs into holiday centerpieces or into a pot of spring flowering (or forced) bulbs.

WALL-HUNG EGG RACKS

Display your handiwork in an attractive collector's rack. You can make your own from scratch or by using pre-cut pieces available in craft shops.

1. If shelves are not precut, measure them to fit the plaque and mark where they are to be cut. Allow 3 inches between each egg shelf and from the top shelf to the top of the plaque. Allow an inch or two of plaque to extend beneath the lowest shelf. A plaque approximately 12 inches square will hold three rows of four eggs.

   Draw 1½ inch diameter circles on the shelves where the egg holes are to be.

2. Cut out the shelves and sand all edges smooth. Use a drill to make a hole in each of the circles. Enlarge the hole with the drill until the opening is large enough to insert the jigsaw. Sand the edges of the hole smooth.

3. Measure and mark the position of the shelves on the plaque. Drill holes through the back of the plaque for screws.

4. Drill corresponding holes in the back side of each shelf.

5. Apply glue to the back edges of each shelf, position in place, and fasten screws through the predrilled holes. Make certain the shelves fit perpendicular to the plaque.

6. Allow glue to dry, paint and decorate egg rack. When the decorations are dry, apply a coat of finish.

7. When all coats are dry, attach picture hanging kit, and mount on the wall.

To make, gather:

Pre-cut, beveled plaque in the size and shape of your choice. (Or, cut and router a ½-inch thick piece of plywood or other board and sand smooth.)

Pre-cut shelves or shelving material

Jig saw to cut shelves and egg holes

Drill

Sandpaper

Screws and screwdriver

Ruler and pencil

Picture hanging kit

Glue

Paints and brushes

Varnish or other finish

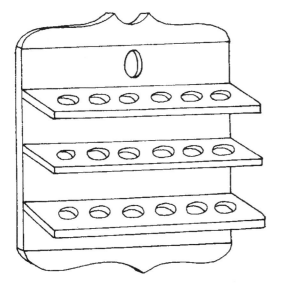

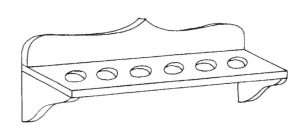

EGGHOLDERS

Craft, candle and general stores carry a range of things that make attractive single eggholders. A quick glance through your cupboards may turn up several acceptable stands for displaying individual eggs. Here are a few to consider:

◆ Candle holders

◆ Small glasses or brandy snifter or shot glasses

◆ Tea or espresso cups

◆ Egg cups (the type used to serve eggs for breakfast)

◆ Doll furniture

◆ Miniature wreaths or nests (from craft shops)

◆ Decorative egg stands (available from Ukrainian gift shops and many shops that cater to egg collectors or decorators)

STAND-UPS

If you are simply looking for a way to set an egg on its end and not have it rock to one side, there are many ways of stabilizing these born-to-rockers.

◆ Push a tack through a piece of cardboard and impale the egg through the blow hole.

◆ Glue a small piece of stiff paper or cardboard to the bottom of the egg.

◆ Glue a ring of yarn or string around the bottom of the egg.

◆ Set or glue egg on a napkin or shower curtain ring.

◆ Cut a ¾-inch piece of toilet paper or paper towel roll, paint or wrap in foil, velvet, etc. to decorate.

◆ Glue a strip of construction paper into a ring or cut a circle of paper, cut a double cross in the center and bend the pieces upwards and glue to egg, like a tiny crown (at the wrong end).

◆ Stitch a strip of starched lace or ribbon into a ring and rest the egg on top.

SAFE KEEPING

Keep some safety tips in mind for the welfare of your precious keepsakes. Don't display over a fireplace or woodstove, rising heat may cause cracks and smoke can damage the finish. Do not keep in direct sunlight as the colors will fade. Store in a place that will not tempt little hands. Glass fronted, or other airtight, display cases, however, are not recommended as the eggs continue to dry out inside over an extended period and require air circulation.

Eggs can be put away each year and brought out to be enjoyed the following season for generations. The best storage container for eggs is a cardboard egg carton. Place the eggs in the individual spaces, close the carton, wrap with a rubber band, and place the carton in a shoebox lined with shredded paper, batting, popcorn, or other packing material for long-term storage. Remember not to store in an airtight container, such as a covered plastic container or plastic bags.

EGGSHELL MOLDS

dd flair to gift baskets or that eggs-stra special touch to Easter parties or get-togethers with egg-shaped novelties. Empty raw eggs into a bowl, and use for cooking (in recipes that do not require separated eggs). One-quarter cup egg contents is approximately equal to one average egg. Cover the shelled eggs tightly and store in the refrigerator.

CHAPTER 15

EGG CANDLES

Brightly colored, carved, or decorated egg-shaped candles are easy to make and are wonderful to include in gift baskets or holiday centerpieces.

To make, gather:

Raw eggs

Manicure scissors

Egg carton

Wax: paraffin, beeswax, or a mixture

Throw-away containers, such as old soup cans, for each color of wax to be used

Color crayons or candle-making dye

Small, metal measuring cup

Large pan

Candle wicking

Wooden spoon or stick to stir wax

Ice pick, straight piece of wire, clothes hanger or long nail to make wick hole

Candle flame or lighter to heat ice pick

CANDLE DYEING

Another way to color egg candles is to omit the crayon melting step and dip the finished candles into a hot dye-bath using an extra-long wick as a handle. When the egg is dry, trim the wick.

1. Prepare eggshell molds by piercing a small hole in the narrow end of the shell with the tip of the manicure scissors and cutting out a hole, about the size of a nickel. Shake the contents into a bowl and reserve for later use. Thoroughly rinse the inside of each egg with warm water, then place the hollow shell, open end down, in an egg carton, and let dry thoroughly.

2. Fill a large pan with an inch or two of water, and bring to a gentle boil. Break up wax to speed melting, place in a throw-away container, and set the container into the hot water. Use a wooden spoon or stick to stir the wax to facilitate smooth, even melting.

3. Wax can be colored at this stage by stirring in broken bits of color crayon until the wax is evenly colored. One crayon will color a quart of wax. One quart of melted wax should fill about 16 eggshells. When the wax is melted and uniformly colored, remove the melted-wax container from heat.

4. Turn eggshells over so that the open end is facing up. Line the egg carton with plastic wrap or aluminum foil and place the upright eggs inside.

5. Pour hot wax into measuring cup, and carefully pour into the eggshells. The wax will condense somewhat as it

cools, making it necessary to top off the eggs after an hour or so. Otherwise you may be going to all this trouble to make Half-Egg Candles. Reserve some wax to fill wick holes. Let the wax eggs set overnight in a warm, draft-free spot.

6. Once the wax has hardened, you are ready to unveil your creation. Gently roll the egg on a tabletop or other hard surface to break the shell. Peel the shell away, being careful not to scratch or gouge the wax beneath.

7. To insert a wick, pierce a wick hole straight through the wax egg with an ice pick heated by candle flame or hand-held lighter. A straight piece of stiff wire or long nail will work too. (This is not a job for kids.) Quickly and carefully force it straight through the egg from one end to the other. Thread a piece of wick through the hole (wax-coated heavy household string will do in a pinch), and place each egg back into the egg carton, lined with plastic wrap or aluminum foil. Reheat reserved wax, pour into measuring cup, and fill the wick holes, being careful not to let hot wax spill onto the sides of the candles. Let the wax harden before continuing to decorate. When dry, trim the wick from the bottom and to about ¾-inch on top.

Layered Egg Candles

Follow all directions as for egg candles, but prepare two or more colors of wax. Pour the first color in, filling only a portion of the eggshell, and allow to dry thoroughly, from 3 to 5 hours. Then pour in a second color to create a layered effect. Allow this layer to harden completely before pouring in the next and so on. The result will be a layered or striped egg, with clear distinct lines of demarcation between each shade. If you wish the colors to flow together, blending where the different shades of wax meet, let the first color harden only partially before pouring in the next shade.

Layers can be formed horizontally by letting the eggs rest upright in a lined egg carton or angled by tilting the egg mold as the wax cools. By tilting the eggshell in different directions for each layer of wax, you can make angled layers in different directions.

Carved Egg Candles

Make egg candles of a solid color, and lightly draw or etch a simple design onto the wax surface. Use a small, sharp knife to carve the design into the wax for a three-dimensional design.

Decorated Egg Candles

Egg candles can be decorated in many of the same ways as genuine eggs. Paint or stencil, or appliqué with small formed pieces of wax, such as hearts or flowers. The candles can be découpaged, either with paper cut-outs or real leaves, flowers, or grasses for an exceptionally pretty look. To decorate egg candles with fresh or dried flowers, the flowers must first be pressed. Place them between two layers of heavy brown paper, such as grocery bags are made from, and press on a hard, solid surface, such as a countertop, with a warm iron. Brush melted, colorless wax onto the egg candle in the areas to be decorated with an artist's paintbrush and gently press the flattened flowers into the warm wax. Paint a coat of wax over the flowers, let dry and repeat with more coats of clear wax until the flowers are totally covered. Although candles decorated in such a fashion are not meant to be burned all the way down, they may be, but the flowers, or découpage pieces will dry and curl and ruin the appearance.

EGG SOAPS

Clean up your gift-giving list with homemade, sweet-smelling egg-shaped soaps. The soaps may be wrapped in colored foil for a bright gift. Here are two easy soap recipes to try.

Clear, Scented Soap

To make, gather:

6 to 8 ounces (2 bars) unscented glycerin soap

½ teaspoon essential-oil fragrance (available at drug stores)

Food coloring

Double boiler, or a small pan or bowl placed inside a large pan.

Whisk or fork

Raw eggs

Egg carton

1. Cut a hole in the top of each egg and empty out and dry, as described on pages 73–74.

2. Cut the bars of soap into small pieces, and melt over boiling water in the top of the double boiler.

3. Add fragrance and a few drops of food coloring, and blend thoroughly with a wire whisk or fork.

4. Carefully fill eggshells (mixture should fill 3 to 4 eggs), and place an egg carton in the refrigerator. Let cool several hours.

5. Gently roll the eggshells to break them up and peel the shell away from the soaps. Soaps may be carved for decoration in the same way as for candles, or left whole. Wrap eggs in crepe tissue paper or colored foil.

Bath Oil Soap

To make, gather:

6 to 8 ounces (two bars) of unscented soap, such as Ivory or Dove

2 cups water

1 tablespoon safflower or other vegetable oil

½ teaspoon essential-oil fragrance

Food coloring

Double boiler, as above

Whisk or fork

Raw eggs

Egg carton

1. Cut a hole in the top of each egg, empty and dry, as described on pages 73–74.

2. Cut the bars of soap into pieces, and melt in double boiler, stirring with whisk or fork until smooth. Run through a blender if lumps persist.

3. Add oil, fragrance, and a few drops of food coloring as desired, and blend with whisk or fork.

4. Carefully pour soap mixture into eggshells. Set the eggs in the egg carton, and cool in the refrigerator.

5. Roll eggshells on countertop to break them, and remove the shells from soaps. Wrap soaps in paper or foil.

CHOCOLATE EGGS

Make this the year you make your own solid chocolate eggs. The secret to great tasting chocolate eggs is to start with your favorite chocolate bar.

1. Prepare eggs by cutting a hole in the top with manicure scissors, emptying the contents out and turning the eggs upside down over paper towels to dry.

2. When the shells are thoroughly dry, dust with corn starch and set them, open end up into the egg carton.

3. Slowly melt the chocolate in the double boiler, or over hot water, or in a microwave at a low setting. Carefully pour into the eggshell molds and let cool in the refrigerator until the chocolate hardens.

To make, gather:

Raw eggs

Manicure scissors

Double boiler, or a small pan placed inside a larger pan

Egg carton

Chocolate bars or milk chocolate chips

Corn starch

EGG CAKES

Covered with Petit Four Glaze (see below) and decorated with icing or sprinkles, these little treasures make the perfect Easter dessert.

1. Empty eggshells, as described on pages 73–74.

2. Prepare cake mix according to recipe.

3. Spoon cake mix into eggshells, until each is about ⅔ full. Use a toothpick or needle to poke a hole into the egg membrane at the bottom of the shell so that it doesn't bubble up while the batter bakes and cause a dip in the egg cake to form.

4. Place the eggs in the wells of the muffin tin. Mini-muffin tins will hold eggs upright, but regular-sized tin wells let the eggs tip over onto their sides unless they are stabilized. A tablespoon or two of rice sprinkled into the bottom of each well will hold the eggs in place.

5. Bake per cake mix instructions for cupcakes.

6. Let the egg cakes cool, then carefully pull the eggshell off in pieces.

7. Dip the egg-shaped cakes in the glaze, then decorate with shaped marzipan, decorative icing, or sprinkles.

To make, gather:

Mini-muffin tin or regular muffin tin and rice

Raw eggs

Cake mix

Petit Four Glaze as follows:

    1 cup powdered sugar

    2 tablespoons hot milk

    ¼ teaspoon vanilla

    Combine and stir until smooth.

Marzipan or decorative icing with tube and tips

Sprinkles

GELATIN EGGS

Wiggly, jiggly, and filled with flavorful fun, these special Easter treats will bring gobs of giggles.

To make, gather:

Raw eggs

Manicure scissors

Egg carton

Gelatin package

1. Hollow eggshells, as described on pages 73–74.

2. Prepare gelatin according to package directions for molds or jigglers.

3. Pour gelatin mixture into eggs, set eggs in carton and cool several hours in the refrigerator.

4. Run warm water over the egg for a few seconds to loosen the shell. Tap eggs to break up shells, and carefully peel from the gelatin eggs.

Variation: Make layered eggs by pouring in only a portion of one kind of gelatin, allowing it to set and then pouring in a second (up to a third) layer of another flavor, in different colors. Layers can be made horizontal by letting the gelatin set with the eggs upright in the cartons or angled by tilting the eggs as the gelatin sets.

ICE EGGS

Even the punch bowl can get into the act with egg-shaped ice ovals.

To make, gather:

Raw eggs

Egg carton

Manicure scissors

Water food coloring (optional)

1. Empty eggs, as described on pages 73–74.

2. Pour water into each eggshell, filling three-quarters of the way full. Place the eggs upright in the carton and freeze.

3. When eggs are frozen solid, run warm water over each for a few seconds to loosen the shell, then peel the pieces away from the ice.

Variation: Add a few drops of food coloring to the water and mix in thoroughly for "dyed" ice eggs.

EGG-CICLES

Give the kids a sweet treat without all the processed sugar. Nutritious, flavorful, and colorful — fruit juices make a great egg-on-a-stick treat.

To make, gather:

Raw eggs

Manicure scissors

Fruit juice, assorted flavors

Egg carton

1. Proceed as for ice eggs. After ice begins to form, push a craft stick or tongue depressor into the hole at the top of each egg. Let freeze and finish as for ice eggs.

EASTER EGGS — BY THE DOZENS!

APPENDIX

SOURCES OF EGG SUPPLIES

Ukrainian Gift Shop, Inc.
2422 Central Ave. NE
Minneapolis, MN 55418
(612) 788-2545
   Aniline Egg Dyes
   Beeswax
   Kistky
      Delrin
      Traditional
      Electric
      Electric with interchange-
         able tips
   Pysanka Poster
   Pysanka Books
   Finished Pysanky
   Egg stands and holders

Eggs Bernadette
Bernadette Wagner
7915N Sharpsburg Ct.
Spokane, WA 99208
      Ukranian and leaf decorated eggs
      Pysanky lessons or contact your
         local art school

Peerless-Sunpuft
N1107 Pearl
Spokane, WA 99202
(509) 328-2672
      Sugar Shell Egg Molds
      Other Easter Candy Molds

OTHER BOOKS YOU MIGHT ENJOY

Bodger, Lorraine and Ephron, Delia. *Crafts for All Seasons.* New York: Universe Books, 1980.

Cohen, Daniel and Paula. *Marbling on Fabric.* Loveland, CO: Interweave Press, 1990.

Coskey, Evelyn. *Easter Eggs for Everyone.* New York: Abingdon Press, 1973.

Herder, K.G. *Decorating Eggs.* New York: Herder and Herder, 1968.

Kramer, Jack. *Natural Dyes, Plants and Processes.* New York: Charles Scribner's Sons, 1972.

Luciow, Johanna; Kmit, Ann and Harrison, Lorreta Luciow. *Eggs Beautiful: How to Make Ukrainian Easter Eggs.* Minneapolis: Smith-Lind Press, 1975.

Newall, Venetia. *An Egg at Easter: A Folklore Study.* London: Routledge & Kegan Paul, 1971.

INDEX